IF THERE IS SUCH A THING AS PURE DESIGN, I DON'T KNOW WHAT IT IS.
I NEED A PROBLEM, A CONTEXT. LIKE AN ACTOR, I HAVE TO CREATE A PROBLEM.

ALAN BUCHSBAUM
ARCHITECT & DESIGNER

ALAN BUCHSBAUM
ARCHITECT & DESIGNER

THE MECHANICS OF TASTE

Edited and introduced by Frederic Schwartz

with essays by
Patricia Leigh Brown
Steven Holl
Rosalind Krauss
Michael Sorkin
Stephen Tilly

THE MONACELLI PRESS

First published in the United States of America in 1996 by
The Monacelli Press, Inc.,
10 East 92nd Street, New York, New York 10128.

Library of Congress Cataloging-in-Publication Data
Alan Buchsbaum, architect & designer : the mechanics of taste / edited and introduced by
Frederic Schwartz ; with essays by Patricia Leigh Brown . . . [et al.].
p. cm.
Includes bibliographical references.
ISBN 1-885254-39-3 (hardcover)
1. Buchsbaum, Alan, 1935–1987—Criticism and interpretation. 2. Architecture, Modern—
20th century—United States. 3. Design—United States—History—20th century.
I. Schwartz, Frederic. II. Brown, Patricia Leigh.
NA737.B755A9 1996
720'.92—dc20   96-22041

Printed and bound in Hong Kong

Designed by Kim Shkapich, *Projects and Projections*

to the memory of my friends,
and 5.8 million others (as of July 1, 1996, the United Nations),
whose lives and careers were cut short by AIDS, for their friendship, inspiration, and work

Alan Buchsbaum, 51, *architect and designer*
Savannah, Georgia, September 26, 1935–New York, New York, April 10, 1987

Roger Ferri, 41, *architect and urban designer*
New York, New York, December 13, 1949–New York, New York, November 20, 1991

Scott Weston, 30, *architect and gardener*
Chicago, Illinois, July 30, 1959–Chicago, Illinois, February 19, 1990

All royalties from this book will be donated to AmFAR (American Foundation For Aids Research)
and GMHC (Gay Men's Health Crisis), as specified in Alan Buchsbaum's will.

ACKNOWLEDGMENTS *8*

NOTES ON THE BOOK *9*

10 PROPOSAL FOR THE 1984/85 DESIGN ARTS FELLOWSHIP
(NEA ADVANCED FELLOWSHIP) AT THE AMERICAN ACADEMY IN ROME Alan Buchsbaum

12 Introduction: All Style(s) Frederic Schwartz

17 What's Wrong with these Pictures? Stephen Tilly

BARROON *32*
PAPER POPPY *34*
METAMORPHOSIS *36*
CADO SHOWROOM *40*
GERBER HOUSE *42*
ROSENBERG HOUSE *47*
HAAS APARTMENT *50*
TENENBAUM INTERIORS *52*
LEWIN APARTMENT *56*
FOAM FURNITURE *58*
BATHROOM *59*
HERE COMES TOMORROW *62*
LLOYDS APARTMENT *64*
COHEN INTERIORS *68*

70 **12 GREENE STREET LOFTS** Alan Buchsbaum

KRAUSS LOFT *72*
BUCHSBAUM LOFT 1 *76*
BUCHSBAUM LOFT 2 *83*
MILLER KITCHEN *92*
ABRAMSON INTERIORS *94*
THE PLAY SETTING *96*
TENENBAUM HOUSE *98*
SANJURJO PENTHOUSE *106*

108 Canal Street Surrealism: The Sensibility of Alan Buchsbaum Rosalind Krauss

RESTIVO APARTMENT *116*
HIRSCH KITCHEN *118*

GERBER/ROTHBERG APARTMENT 120
JAKOBSON BEDROOM 126

128   The Divine Mr. B   Patricia Leigh Brown

CHARIVARI MEN'S AND WOMEN'S STORES 134
FILM FORUM 1 136
MOONDANCE DINER 138
GENNARO ANDREOZZI OFFICE 142
6-5-4-3-2-1 WYOMING 144
HEGEL'S VACATION 146
RED 147
PATRICOFF KITCHEN 150
KEATON APARTMENT 152
BALABAN/GROSSMAN APARTMENT 154
BRINKLEY APARTMENT 158
BARKIN LOFT 160
MIDLER LOFT 164
WINTOUR/SHAFFER TOWNHOUSE 172
JOEL/BRINKLEY PENTHOUSE 178
DENNIS APARTMENT 183
WINTOUR TABLE 192
NEVELE CHAIR 193
SUGAR CHAIR 194
ROCK STAR COFFEE TABLE 194
ELKES TABLES 195
O'KEEFE TOWNHOUSE 196

198   Alan Buchsbaum, 1935–1987   Michael Sorkin

ECCO SHOES 202
NEVELE HOTEL LOBBY 204
V'SOSKE RUGS 210

216   Alan Buchsbaum: Personal Recollections   Steven Holl

PROJECT LIST 218
BIBLIOGRAPHY 221

ACKNOWLEDGMENTS

The responsibility of editing the first book on the work of my friend Alan Buchsbaum presented an arduous personal challenge. It is tragic that so often architects do not receive the critical acclaim they deserve until they are gone. I wish especially to thank my friends, sister, and parents for their patience and support over the past eight years.

At Monacelli Press, I am grateful to Andrea Monfried for her sensitivity to Buchsbaum's work, her enthusiasm, and her editorial skills and to Steve Sears for his invaluable production expertise. Above all, I wish to thank the publisher, Gianfranco Monacelli, for his generosity, commitment to this book, and appreciation of Alan Buchsbaum's work. Grazie.

A special thanks to the very talented designer Kim Shkapich for her keen eye and her representation of Buchsbaum's work in type, color, photo, and form. Her collaboration and innovative thinking added an immeasurable layer of meaning to the presentation of his work.

Thanks to Patricia Leigh Brown, Steven Holl, Rosalind Krauss, Michael Sorkin, and Stephen Tilly (a Design Coalition partner) for their enlightening and poignant essays that provide insight into Buchsbaum's work and personality.

Thanks to Buchsbaum's friends Barbara Jakobson, Susan Grant Lewin, and Mark Simon for sharing their reminiscences about their work with Buchsbaum.

I am indebted to the following photographers for their beautiful and spirited images of Buchsbaum's work; without their generous contributions and cooperation this book would not have been possible: Peter Aaron/ESTO, Wesley Balz, Langdon Clay, Elliot Fine, Oberto Gili, David Heinlein, Thomas Hooper, Peter Hujar, Elliott Kaufman, Bill Maris, Norman McGrath, Steve Moore, Michael Mundy, Charles Nesbit, Peter Paige, Joyce Ravid, and Robert Wortham.

While editing this book I have attempted to assemble all known articles and books that refer to Buchsbaum. I especially thank the following writers and editors who consistently and eloquently published his work: Marilyn Bethany, Martin Filler, Vera Graaf, Elaine Greene, Robert Janjigian, Joan Kron, Susan Grant Lewin, Nory Miller, Norma Skurka, Suzanne Slesin, Elizabeth Sverbeyeff Byron, Susan Szenasy, and Anna Wintour.

Thanks to Maggie Mahboubian and Marybeth Shaw for their invaluable assistance in helping to write many of the project descriptions and to Blu Greenberg for her editorial advice.

Thanks to Corey Delany (Buchsbaum's irreplaceable office/life manager and interior design assistant) for her help with research and the bibliography and for providing a steadfast presence during difficult times and to Marc L'Italien (whom Buchsbaum called his "most talented designer in twenty years") for his insights, writing, and friendship.

Thanks to Charles Gandee at Condé Nast for his help in obtaining photographs and for his recognition of Buchsbaum's last projects in a beautifully produced article in Architectural Record written by Martin Filler. Also thanks to Peter Lograsso at Color Wheel Inc. for his help with color reproduction.

The book was written and edited at Buchsbaum's former office in Soho, New York, currently the location of Creative Technologies. I am grateful to Maria Arbusto, Noah Carter, Thomas Lakofski, Jon Oakes, and James Venturi for the use of their office and computer expertise.

My most sincere thanks to Buchsbaum's staff, clients, family, and friends for their insights and stories, including Stanley Abercrombie, Bob Balaban and Lynn Grossman, George Beylerian, Lance Brown, Pat and Allan Dennis, Ruth and Terry Elkes, Lou Gropp, Joan Kron, Bette Midler, Jeffrey Osborne, Larry Panish, Gloria Buchsbaum Smiley, and Charles Thanhauser.

At my office, thanks to Caroline Otto and Elizabeth Alford for their editorial assistance and to Reese Madrid for all her help. Also, thanks to Ross Anderson for "time out," especially during Alan's illness.

A special thanks to Françoise Blanc, Maggie Mahboubian, and Elizabeth Ward for their editing skills, perspective, and encouragement during the difficult days and years following Alan's death.

Finally, thanks to Alan Buchsbaum: for the extraordinary opportunity to write about your work, for your kindness and friendship, and for all that you taught me about design, flowers, and style.

—Frederic Schwartz

"Alan could get you to agree to almost any design and make you feel like it was your idea in the first place. His success stems not only from his enormous talent, but from the fact that he was a shrewd diplomat—Henry Kissinger in a Hawaiian shirt."
—Bob Balaban and Lynn Grossman

NOTES ON THE BOOK

This book illustrates the innovative work of Alan Buchsbaum (and Design Coalition) from 1967 to 1987 —a fast, fun, and evocative period in art, music, design, and the life of America (especially New York), spanning from the psychedelic "summer of love" to the devastation of AIDS. This book is neither a definitive work nor an in-depth academic study. Rather it highlights Buchsbaum's most important projects, which represent his significant contributions to design and illustrate his evolution as an architect during a brief and brilliant career.

Shortly after Buchsbaum passed away I learned that he had left me his firm. His archives included sketches, presentation and construction drawings, photographs, job files, magazine articles, and the notes that provided the majority of material for this book as well as direction for years of research.

The projects illustrated here were selected for their relative importance in exhibiting the diversity and quality of Buchsbaum's work. They are organized in roughly chronological order following his evolution as an architect and representing his major interests— Pop Art and Super-Graphics, "High-Tech," Surrealism, and his own brand of romantic modernism. The order of the work reflects his self-proclaimed non-linear thinking and demonstrates the crossover of his ideas relating to architecture, interiors, and the decorative arts.

We remember Buchsbaum's work most indelibly through photography. He was skilled at persuading editors to pay for photo shoots while allowing him to style the locations. Most of Buchsbaum's early work was well documented and beautifully photographed by Norman McGrath, while the majority of his later work, particularly the residential projects, was elegantly photographed by Oberto Gili.

An accomplished photographer himself, Buchsbaum often captured images and abstractions of natural forms that reinforced his interest in pattern and texture. His photographs of flowers, trees, plants, and clouds were used as the images for his wall-sized super-graphics (pages 92 and 95), installations (pages 144–47), and rugs (pages 105 and 212–13).

Buchsbaum's drawings and sketches are not the emphasis of this book. They are incidental to his achievements, no matter how much we value them now. His work was built from well-detailed construction drawings (often by others) and by his own site-oriented and hands-on approach (for a few years he was a partner in the Greene Street Construction Co.). He was notorious for changing work in the field, and he placed great trust in the abilities of his artisans and fabricators. While there are many construction drawings (page 83) in his archives, there are relatively few free-hand and development drawings. The few remaining sketches exhibit an economy of line and a soft, suggestive, delicate hand (page 27). The varied presentation styles (pages 36, 46–47, 64, and 98) reflect the particular skills of his changing staff; for example, a series of ink-on-mylar cut-away axonometrics, illustrating walls, spaces, and furniture, was drawn by Davis Sprinkle during his stay (page 160). Buchsbaum's own preferred method of presenting floor and furniture plans was to use colored pencil on blue and sepia prints to emphasize the richness of form and composition (pages 142 and 165).

Kim Shkapich's book design reflects the spirit of Buchsbaum's work and methodology; it is pragmatic and arbitrary, constantly shifting scale and adjusting to the information required for each project. Cinematic in concept, the design features small, tight close-ups and wide-angle-like double-page full bleeds. Buchsbaum's voice (for project descriptions and quotes) is highlighted in the font COPPERPLATE GOTHIC 30BC to contrast with the essay text, in the font Simoncini Garamond, and the project description type, Rotis Semi Sans Regular. The title type is **FUTURA BOLD CONDENSED** and the credit type is DIN 1451 Engschrift.

Much work remains to be done in regard to Buchsbaum's oeuvre, especially with respect to the study of his drawings and papers. I hope this book and the selection of projects included will inspire students and scholars to examine his work and life more closely.

—Frederic Schwartz

PROPOSAL FOR THE 1984/85 DESIGN ARTS FELLOWSHIP (NEA ADVANCED FELLOWSHIP) AT THE AMERICAN ACADEMY IN ROME

ALAN BUCHSBAUM

Alan Buchsbaum wrote the following application essay in 1984 describing his interests in collage and illusion:

MY WORK AS AN ARCHITECT HAS BEEN DEVELOPING SINCE 1967, AND HAS INCLUDED COMMERCIAL AND RESIDENTIAL PROJECTS, THEATERS, AND USE STUDIES OF MUNICIPAL SITES, AS WELL AS INTERIORS AND INTERIOR RENOVATIONS THAT ENCOMPASS SPACE PLANNING AND FURNITURE DESIGN. BECAUSE IT JUXTA-POSES MANY UNUSUAL COMBINATIONS OF MATERIALS, COLORS, AND SPACES BEYOND THOSE OF THE NORMAL ARCHITECTURAL VOCABULARY, MY WORK HAS BEEN CHARACTERIZED AS *COLLAGE,* A TERM THAT DEFINES AN AESTHETIC CATEGORY IN WHICH I AM, INDEED, INTERESTED. COLLAGE'S PLAY WITH AND QUESTIONING OF THE NOTION OF THE REAL (REALITY AS AN ABSOLUTE) HAS ALWAYS SEEMED PROMISING TO ME AS A MODEL FOR ARCHI-TECTURAL METHOD. IN SAYING THAT, I AM OBVIOUSLY QUESTION-ING THE NOTION OF ARCHITECTURAL "PURITY," AND IN FACT, MY OWN PRACTICE HAS PROCEEDED BY TAKING SERIOUSLY IDEAS GENERATED OUTSIDE THE WORLD OF ARCHITECTURE, PARTICU-LARLY WITHIN THE VISUAL ARTS, POPULAR CULTURE, THEATER, MUSIC, AND LITERATURE. HOWEVER, I DESIGN INTUITIVELY AND AM INTERESTED IN THE EMOTIONAL EXPERIENCE OF WHICH ARCHITECTURE IS CAPABLE; THEREFORE, I TRY TO DEVELOP SPACES THAT OFFER VISCERAL AS WELL AS VISUAL SATISFAC-TIONS. RATHER THAN DEAL WITH ABSTRACT DESIGN PHILOSOPHY, I HAVE BEEN AN INVENTIVE PRAGMATIST AND AM QUITE GRATI-FIED THAT ALMOST ALL OF MY PROJECTS HAVE BEEN REALIZED.

Joel/Brinkley Penthouse,1985

ALL STYLE(S)

Frederic Schwartz

So peculiar and extraordinary an architect was Alan Buchsbaum that it would be dangerous to classify his work too specifically. Why would one want to? He remains one of the more important and complex figures in the pre-post- and post-modern periods because of his constant change and blurring of roles as architect, designer, and decorator. He does not easily fit into any one place. There is no one style. He is all style(s).

In his eclectic career, spanning two short decades (long for dancers and athletes, short for artists and architects), Buchsbaum designed houses, apartments, lofts, a pinball arcade, shoe stores, offices, kitchens and bathrooms, installations, signage, furniture, wallpaper, rugs, parks, a hotel lobby, a diner, a movie theater, and a disco. In the design world Buchsbaum gradually became legendary, which is to say that almost everyone had heard of him but few could actually tell you what he had designed. Though fiercely respected by a formidable group of writers and editors (especially in New York), his work was too odd and varied to be categorized. He was purposefully elusive but not intentionally obscure. Conventional, pragmatic, and averse to compromise on basic design principles, he rejected straightforward solutions and instead opted for a relaxed and personal approach. He was user-friendly and cost-conscious (especially in kitchens and bathrooms) but could also be aloof. Admiring critics would publish striking images of his work and his succinct zingers because they were bold, cutting-edge, amusing, candid, and made good copy. He was a behind-the-scenes self-promoter and helped as much as anyone to shape his own myth.

It's not easy to be new. What looks common in Buchsbaum's work today was then daring and unorthodox. Over time, his projects (and details) have been so thoroughly absorbed into our memory that it is easy to take him for granted and to confuse him with his followers. While Buchsbaum refused to be overlooked, he was also clear about not identifying himself with any one style or movement. In fact, he held the style-stars and style-makers in contempt. He was too diverse and complicated to be classified before he was on to something new. He fought his own battles to leave behind the comfort associated with familiar fads and challenged the definitions of architecture and design, while others pursued his lead and tried to imitate his style.

> MODERN (1984) EXCLUDES ALL SCIENCES, AND INCLUDES ALL ARTS. IT SUGGESTS CONFUSION, CACOPHONY, PLURALITY OF STYLES, OVERLAPPING IMAGES, QUICKSILVER CHANGES AND NON SEQUITURS. IT'S IMPOSSIBLE TO BELIEVE IN ONE AESTHETIC.

> I WON'T USE A HOLOPHANE LAMP ANYMORE BECAUSE IT'S NOW IN EVERY ICE CREAM STORE IN THE CITY.

Like his work, Buchsbaum himself was a complex juxtaposition, an ambiguous portrait of images, moods, and ideals. He was a sometimes shy, wise-cracking Jew born in Georgia in 1935 who received a science degree from the Georgia Institute of Technology in 1958 and an architectural degree from MIT in 1961, traveled extensively in Japan and Italy, and hiked the Appalachian Trail. After school he worked in New York for Conklin Rossant on the design of the new town center at Reston, Virginia, and then for Warner Burns Toan and Lunde on the design of the Princeton University Mathematics Building. Tired of working at a large office for someone else, Buchsbaum started Design Coalition in 1967. He was the king of kitsch and the master of mundane, an excellent chef and a food critic, a clotheshorse and an interminable gossip, a confidante to beautiful and brilliant women. Buchsbaum was abashedly gay. He wasn't in the closet, but he wasn't exactly out either. He was warm, incredibly intelligent and articulate, edgy, and demanding. When he was on, he had tremendous enthusiasm and a quiet self-confidence, which he imparted to his staff. When he was off, he could be loud, foul-mouthed, and abrasive. Buchsbaum was very proud, determined, and somewhat bitter about not getting the kind of respect or work he thought he deserved.

DESIGN IS COMING OUT OF THE CLOSET IF YOU LIKE, OR RATHER OPENING THE CLOSET DOOR AND REVEALING THE CONTENTS.

Buchsbaum's brilliant and sometimes eccentric work avoided the banalities of repetitive insistence on one style by exploiting the paradoxes and incongruities of the downtown scene. He was a keen observer of his own times, and clients relished his commentary, wit, know-how, and style. He had an inspired point of view that placed equal value on the everyday and the exquisite. Buchsbaum would go to the Bowery to buy a restaurant stool and then to Vienna to find a Josef Hoffman chair. His eye never compromised. He had a fresh way of looking at things and was extraordinarily inventive in his selection and juxtaposition of furniture and objects for his unique architectural settings.

TO BE CREATIVE MEANS TO DO SOMETHING THAT YOU HAVEN'T SEEN BEFORE—SO I CHANGE.

There were many periods and overlapping interests in Buchsbaum's work. The late sixties and early seventies were distinguished as the era in which the spirit of America, largely through its young people, was renewed and revitalized. Buchsbaum's architecture and interiors reflected this spirit; its optimism, vitality, and openness were exhibited in his Super-Graphics and

Pop Art–influenced projects: Metamorphosis, Paper Poppy, Lucidity, CADO, and the Miller Kitchen. Buchsbaum painted rainbows and psychedelic swirls (pages 16 and 35), planted giant roses on kitchen walls (page 92), produced inflatable (page 32) and foam (page 58) furniture, and also designed quirky, contemporary, cubic houses with knotty pine interiors (pages 42–49).

In the mid-seventies, Buchsbaum was credited as one of the leading figures of "High-Tech," combining common off-the-shelf materials with polished details and bold colors. His own lofts at Greene Street (pages 76–91) are collage-like, richly detailed, contrasting the new and the old, palpable with color, fabric, and texture. The pre-AIDS seventies—free love, open sex, gay discos, the New York baths scene—was the context for Buchsbaum's own laboratory-for-design lofts and their programs for almost-public baths in private spaces. In his lofts even the bathrooms and hot tubs are part of the open, "free" plan. Straight life, no matter how bizarre or offbeat, usually falls back on familiar conventions; bathrooms are supposed to have walls and doors—aren't they? But downtown, in Buchsbaum's evolving architecture of lofts, it could all hang out. In his office loft design for Gennaro Andreozzi, all hell breaks loose (pages 142–43). Everything is slightly and purposefully off-key, just enough to set you on edge. These projects exhibit depth and sophistication, demonstrating Buchsbaum's command of plan, materials, and composition mixed with new energy and abandon. He defined the architecture of lofts as free-flowing modern space with occasional rooms for privacy. After a while, even the uptown crowd longed for his downtown style.

In the early eighties Buchsbaum continued his experimentation and exhibited an interest in Surrealism and stage sets. In the Restivo Apartment (pages 116–17) and his two Casa Tile installations (pages 144–47), he registered his disdain for any expectation of realism by producing settings of dreamlike fantasy through an economical juxtaposition of materials and theatrical techniques.

As Buchsbaum's work matured, he developed his own brand of cool, romantic modernism, rich in materials and textures, and particularly evident in a series of cutting-edge lofts and apartments for his demanding, intelligent clients: Bill Gerber and Arlene Rothberg, Diane Keaton, Bob Balaban and Lynn Grossman, Ellen Barkin, Bette Midler, Anna Wintour and David Schaffer, Billy Joel and Christie Brinkley, and Pat and Allan Dennis (pages 152–91). In this later work the disparate themes are organized into a delicate balance of space, light, color, and furnishing. The whole is much greater than the sum of his many parts. The elements of high- and low-tech were pared down into polished details and set against juxtapositions of new

WHEN I SAY I DON'T THINK I HAVE A STYLE, I AM SAYING THAT I AM HAPPY THAT LOTS OF THINGS APPEAL TO ME—THAT I CAN ADAPT.

and old, conventional and extraordinary. His earlier use of bold colors run riot was controlled and placed against subtle and neutral backgrounds. He was in demand, his clients were famous, his materials (and budgets) became richer; Buchsbaum became more refined. In his townhouse design for Anna Wintour and David Schaffer his work started to look effortless, so appropriate and so elegant that one could not imagine ever designing something more beautiful. Its poetry conveys what words cannot. Editors, architects, and decorators waited for his next move. He was at the top of his game. And then there was AIDS.

I became good friends with Buchsbaum when I returned from the American Academy in Rome in 1985 and he rented me the raw fourth-floor loft at 12 Greene Street on a month-to-month basis with the promise that I would leave on no notice. Almost every morning on my way to work, I would drop by Alan's office for our own kind of "coffee talk." As with many of his other friends, he would tell me the joke of the day and some sworn-to-secrecy gossip about one of his star-friends. Sometimes I would go with him to buy flowers and visit one of his projects. A few months later Alan started catching lingering colds, and then the colds became pneumonia, and then he became ill. And then he became very ill. AIDS suggested a new clock, with no numbers, with hands running wildly out of control, a clock where every minute counted and the alarm was always ringing. I remember my mother telling me then that "time moves fast as it seems to stand still."

I worked with Alan Buchsbaum and his office during his last year, when he asked if I would complete his ongoing projects and assist him with new ones. He was very clear and up front with prospective clients; he wanted to keep working and offered assurances (me) that the work would be completed. He had a new disease, and we didn't exactly know its full implications. The inevitability of his death loomed over us. Through it all, the work continued, and whenever he was strong enough, he was back on the job.

Buchsbaum's clients were understanding, compassionate, and more than ready to go forward. I refer especially to Michael O'Keefe, Pat and Allan Dennis, and Robert and Arlene Kogod. I would work every morning at Buchsbaum's office with his exceptionally talented staff, Corey Delany, Marc L'Italien, and Jaime Vasquez; in the afternoon at my office; and evenings if Alan was in the hospital, I would visit him. If he was well enough, we would talk about work. If not, he would moan, complain about the food, and ask when he could go home. Never one to lose his sense of humor, Alan joked that the multicolored tubes sprouting haphazardly from his body made it look like the Beaubourg in Paris (a favorite building of his)—tragedy and comedy rolled up into one.

It was not a good time. AIDS was on the front page of the *New York Times* almost every day and was the cover story for both *Time* and *Newsweek* (Alan's picture was on the cover among a mosaic of one hundred other prominent artists). The stigma attached to this mysterious, savage virus and the toll it took on Alan's body and spirit were unimaginable. Frantic calls came from all over with news of the latest cures and natural remedies. Nothing worked. Buchsbaum died on April 10, 1987, at the age of 51. His tragic death, like more than 5.8 million others (and counting), remains inexplicable.

On April 24, 1987, a memorial, attended by a crowd of hundreds, was held at Metro Pictures, a Soho art gallery up the block from Buchsbaum's home and office on Greene Street. Michael Sorkin, Martin Filler, Rosalind Krauss, and others paid moving tributes by presenting slides of his work. His family and friends recalled happier days. We laughed a little and cried a lot. Mandy Patinkin played the piano and sang one of Alan's favorite songs, "Sonny Boy." Bette Midler closed the "show" and sang the "The Rose." Alan would have loved it. The rose—bold and subtle, soft and cutting, simple and complex—was a perfect metaphor for Buchsbaum and his own style(s) of modernism.

WHAT'S WRONG WITH THESE PICTURES?

Stephen Tilly

Flowers

On August 10 of last year an over-achieving night-blooming *Epiphyllum* plant, removed from dim loft living to our greenhouse by Alan ten years ago, produced four huge, spiky, Busby Berkeley–esque blooms whose heavy perfume announced the action yards away. These flamboyant, over-the-top exotics last just one night and in the morning are the embodiment of the word *spent.* Alan's appetite for this excitement was ahead of his ability patiently to nurture these odd gangly cacti, and pot after pot arrived from Greene Street.

   Cut flowers were more amenable to Alan's way of life. He was a frequent customer at the flower market, at dawn before a photo shoot, a dinner party, or just another workday. For Alan, sensory deprivation was truly an oxymoron. Flowers, food, smells, and a wild variety of shapes and textures found their way into his own living space as well as those he designed for others. Images blurred into spaces; we (and our clients) found ourselves inhabiting (or trying to) a sensuous image: the huge rose that consumed an entire wall in the Miller kitchen (page 92); Bette Midler's onyx gingko-leaf sink top (above); the tree branches in the Tenenbaum House carpet (page 105); the "Serious Leaves" rug for V'Soske (page 212); the VIP room at Metamorphosis (opposite); Alan's splash-shaped Jacuzzi (page 91); and the curving glass block and runway lights of the third floor loft on Greene Street (page 77), to which we moved from our office uptown in 1976.

Starting Out

We laid out the glass block curve and responding squiggly countertop on the spot with a garden hose, roughly following a plan drawn up in the office we shared with several architects and a graphic designer in a converted stable on Thirty-fifth Street in midtown Manhattan.

   I had started there with Alan in the mid-seventies, when Design Coalition had dwindled to just him. When he ran out of money to pay me as an employee, he made me his partner, a gesture with a typical Buchsbaum mixture of savvy, generosity, and impatience.

When I began working with Alan he was doing colorful, stream-lined stuff, glossy, patterned, and with lots of curves. He loved stone, and at that time it was usually highly polished and often curvilinear. Mirrors and tile added more gloss, softened sometimes by mohair and leather furniture, usually Italian, often Bellini or Magistretti. Italian influence notwithstanding, and he was always an Italophile, Alan some-times called this his "Jewish modern" or, alternately, "high tack" phase. The jobs were apartment renovations, kitchens, and bathrooms, a few stores and agencies, all the staples of small New York design practices, especially in the profession's perennial recession. Alan's occasional slowly drawled question was, STEVE, IS THIS SIGNIFICANT ARCHITECTURE?

Social—but Useful?

Alan's irony set off real resonances in my head. I landed on Thirty-fifth Street a recent émigré from the politically charged atmosphere of Cambridge and Boston during the late sixties and early seventies, where I had studied, demonstrated, organized, designed, carpentered, stood on unemployment lines, and researched and carried out participatory plan-ning projects with colleagues and ideological descendants of MIT city planner Kevin Lynch.

Unemployed again after a brief stint in Paul Friedberg's window-less landscape studio on Sixty-third Street, I met a planning colleague from Cambridge who had worked with Alan at Conklin Rossant and had been in touch with him recently. He said Alan was a great guy, an interesting designer, but added that he didn't necessarily respect the kind of work Alan was doing. He didn't explain but I later realized he was referring to the social utility of Alan's projects. Charivari clothing stores and lacquered media walls did seem a long way from planning downtown Washington or designing a Boston subway station with "user consultants." Still, there was clear non-mainstream, if not anti-establish-ment, flavor to the enterprise, beyond the beard and Hawaiian shirts. I continued throughout our joint practice to direct energies to socially "useful" projects, working on playgrounds and public space and school-ing myself in solar and energy-conserving design. At the same time I slowly realized there was much to learn from our bread-and-butter resi-dential and commercial work, more substance than the slick surfaces sometimes suggested.

Superficiality

It was in fact the surfaces that conveyed the news: making spaces is about making surfaces. Changing the material—altering its texture, reflectiveness, apparent depth, color, acoustical properties, or even its cultural associations—changes the space. An ancient message, perhaps, but it was just sinking in for me. Though he could do inventive layouts, Alan got most excited about the materials he used and celebrated them, sometimes to a fault. This way of working was superficial, in the best sense. Our offices were experiments with vast collections of materials. The conference rooms on Greene Street were full of samples: metals, marbles, onyx, fabrics, carpet strike-offs, laminates, and paint chips filled shelves and cabinets and hung on the walls. I had always been excited by structure and space, but this immersion in the immediacy of the surface was a revelation. As slow and ponderous as the design and construction process was, this way of working was somehow like painting: mucking around in the materials, distressing them, polishing them, trying them out next to each other in new ways.

Design/Build Coalition

Adding to this effect was the fact that our process of getting projects built was very hands-on, not long on documentation, and full of discussions, arguments, and screaming shit-fits with contractors, suppliers, and even clients. Having been a designer and contractor more than a draftsman, I was comfortable with this approach. Alan did wonderful design drawings but often skimped on the construction document side, sometimes pulling unfinished sheets off the boards when time or money ran out. Since most of the work was indoors, we weren't forced to detail for the weather and had great freedom to try special effects, sort of like working in California, but without the earthquakes and mudslides.

For many jobs we were de facto general contractors, often using the same masons, carpenters, plumbers, and painters, and an electrician we had trained in the special manipulations required to hang a Holophane pendant light or mount a sandblasted and lacquered Abolite fixture. We charged 25 percent of the cost and didn't (to my knowledge) make a lot of money. Alan may have had limited technical expertise, but he could get contractors to build what he wanted. Sometimes it required going ballistic, and Alan was always good at that. In person or on the phone he could crescendo mid-sentence to a shout. Contractors we worked with often, like Nick and Pete Charalambous, would tell stories of their explosive encounters to me. On our end, we would practice Nick and Pete imitations ("extra work, extra work, all the time, extra work"). Between Alan's temper and comments like "Who does your hair, Con Ed?" made by an employee to a particularly distracted, frizzy receptionist, we went through a lot of support staff, until Alan found Corey Delany, who became more an invaluable administrative partner than a staff person.

Alan's unwillingness to suffer fools gladly meant he was unlikely to roll with mistakes or willful misunderstandings by contractors or employees, and it also meant we often got a better product. I was more of a good cop and sometimes, to my dismay, cast in the role of the solid, grounded technocrat. When the *Times* did a piece on fancy bathrooms, they talked to Alan about nudity and to me about humidity.

OUR WHOLE FEELING ABOUT NUDITY HAS CHANGED. THE RATIONALE SEEMS TO BE THAT IF YOU'RE FRIENDLY ENOUGH TO LIVE WITH SOMEBODY, THEN IT'S NOT TOO FAR-FETCHED TO BATHE IN FRONT OF THEM.

Alan stayed away from clients and projects he didn't like or found boring, rather than trying to find a way to be of service. There were still the usual clients from hell, and relationships that soured midstream. As difficult as those situations were, they also led to some Keystone Kops episodes savored in the office, like Alan's late-night escape through closing subway doors from a friend/client turned enemy/client who was sitting nearby. There were some lean years, but he didn't wind up wasting a lot of time just keeping the doors open or solving clients' problems. He always found a way to try something out, to fabricate style, to conjure up even one arresting photo op. He looked for clients who wanted his funky approach, who connected with his vision and even improved on it. He talked, for example, about how wonderful it was to work with Bill Gerber and Arlene Rothberg (who introduced him to Diane Keaton), because they had taste and it showed in their space, in the objects they chose and the way they art-directed their surroundings (pages 120–25).

Design Coalition

Among my records is a Design Coalition brochure (below) from the early seventies, before my time. Design Coalition is in punchy white letters on a black six-by-eight-inch cover, and on the back the cover is duplicated backwards, as if the pamphlet were transparent. This witticism may have

come from the Coalition, but the humor and self-deprecation of the work have a Buchsbaum ring. Graphically, the piece shares a sensibility with the flying eagle of Alan's later solo logo (page 31) and the torn paper logo of Greene Street Construction, a contracting firm Alan started with David Becker, a young painter who did construction to make a living. We adopted the same backwards approach to our own report and proposal covers, which were in the subtle seventies color scheme inherited from the previous era: white on pumpkin orange.

The other members of the early Coalition, which was "organized in 1967" according to the brochure, were two architects, Howard Korenstein and Rosario Piomelli, whom Alan had met while working in other offices in the city, and a graphic designer, Alan Mitelman. Rosario had joined the group after its founding, adding her portfolio of solid sixties institutional work to the aggressive geometrics and swirling super-graphics of the groups' completed projects. After I arrived I got to know the earlier Design Coalition projects by talking to prospective clients and showing them slides of the work.

One of the first projects, Metamorphosis (pages 16, 36–39), was two stores in one, a men's boutique tucked inside sweeping curves separating it from its brother/sister, a hair salon. The glazing openings are giant stylized heads, back to back, with parallel angled glazed doors as necks. Bright colors and semicircles are everywhere: lettering, furniture, hairdryers, walls, super-graphics. Other stores picked up the same sock-it-to-you theme.

The Gerber House in Chappaqua (below and pages 42–46) was a neat, vertically sided, cubic package enclosing a typical family program and a swimming pool. I assume Howard Korenstein designed the enclosure, since that is how we later divided responsibilities. Inside, Alan's hand is evident—if not hyper-evident. The plastic-covered plywood walls around the pool shimmer with reflected light and polychrome super-murals, including a stack of giant 3-D Lifesavers, across from a ten-foot graphic painted on the opposite wall, a head-shaped splash pattern (precursor of his own "splash" hot tub), which looks like Hirschfeld on acid. A pair of Alan's inflatable chairs hovers outside the pool enclosure on the deck, and upstairs, plastic furniture shares tiled floors with a few plants and PVC tube floor lamps. Modern, but definitely not minimal.

The Big Pictures

By the mid-seventies when I arrived at Thirty-fifth Street, the super-graphics in the slide show had started to look a little tired, and Alan's design interests had moved on. He no longer did super-graphics in the sixties sense, but he was intrigued by jolting changes of scale like those produced by 3M murals. We played around a lot with the 3M process and other ways of introducing images at an architectural scale, an idea Alan pursued later in the series of rugs made by V'Soske from photo enlargements (pages 210–15).

Just Plain Tech: 12 Greene Street

The work was evolving as we planned Alan's new loft on the third floor of 12 Greene Street (pages 76–82). While the details, materials, and ideas wound up peppered throughout Joan Kron and Suzanne Slesin's classic book *High-Tech,* the tech was not really that high at all. If one was hermit-crabbing a residence or office inside a wide-open industrial shell, why not use industrial and commercial equipment, whose design was often flat-out functional and good-looking to boot? Ours was the tech of the factory purchasing agent's catalogs, of building and restaurant supply stores on Canal Street and the Bowery; it required connoisseurship but not complex technical chops. It was *not* the tech of Ove Arup, Norman Foster, Bucky Fuller, or the space shuttle.

Alan bought the building with his friends Rosalind Krauss, the art historian and critic, and Robert Morris, the artist. Alan had helped Bob with a studio in the country and was instrumental in getting the necessary work done on the Soho building. In particular, he helped Rosalind put together her loft, a serene white space proclaimed in a *New Yorker* piece as one of the most beautiful in Manhattan (pages 72–75), and his own office/residence (right). That first loft was an opportunity for Alan to plan space, his own space, with great freedom. The constraints were four walls with a center line of columns instead of the more restrictive, cramped confines of an apartment house. The S-curve of the glass-block wall is a manifesto of the free line—not tied to anything else. In order to be able to build this essay at all, Alan parlayed potential publication into free and discounted materials: tile, glass block, paint, wire shelves. We became dealers of a line of low-end laminate cabinets and used those whenever possible. Necessity gave its proverbial motherly assist to this enlargement of the realm of objects that could live together in the same space, and there were provocative new juxtapositions. The luscious polished marble top accentuated the straightforward design strength of the industrial light fixture, and the metal fixture (and the light it produced) in turn emphasized by contrast the sleek perfection and rich color of the marble.

Soho was the perfect place to look for raw materials. There were still more manufacturers than art dealers and good stuff was everywhere. Canal Street between the office and the subway was a cornucopia of plastics, metals, office equipment, and surplus anything. We always wanted to do an entire project using only materials available on Greene Street, including moving quilts, brass, industrial shelving, recycled rags, hardware, brooms, paint, crates, etc.

Exploring such new territory is exciting, but when designers and architects show up in the neighborhood, gentrification has begun. With the book *High-Tech* as a guide, great masses followed Alan, Paul Marantz, Joe D'Urso, and a host of practical loft dwellers to restaurant supply houses, wholesale shelving dealers, hospital equipment suppliers, and marine hardware stores. It was clear this trend had peaked when Holophane put out its watered-down residential fixtures and they started lighting ferns in restaurants and malls across the country.

Sidelines

Alan cultivated other ventures on the sidelines, like inflatable furniture (pages 32–33) and the contracting company mentioned earlier. Acme

Diary Company produced a crisp square appointment calendar with the year in raised vacuum-formed hot-dog letters on the plastic cover. Free Acme diaries (at least until 1980), like fabulous leftovers, good shelter-press gossip, free eats with FAT (Alan's *Village Voice* food critic persona), and recipe testing of his friend Colette Rossant's food-processor cookbook, were the fringe benefits at Design Coalition.

He was famous for staying in touch with editors: Suzanne Slesin, Joan Kron, Susan Lewin, Marilyn Bethany, Suzanne Stephens, Lou Gropp, Stanley Abercrombie, Anna Wintour—the list goes on and on. The king of schmooze, he cackled, whispered, cajoled, spread the word; and he threw great dinner parties. He was an accomplished cook and a generous host. His lofts looked best at night, when his attention to lighting effects (and that of lighting designer Paul Marantz and others) paid off handsomely. In the first loft on Greene Street, the street-side furniture grouping, mostly freebie leftovers from a furniture showroom design job, was not terribly comfortable. Dinner guests sat, without back support, on a carpeted platform with a foot well (the dining pit) around a gorgeous round *rosa* marble table (right). A wall piece in folded industrial felt by Robert Morris hung behind the table. Our

souped-up Italian drafting boards stood nearby in twilight. Few seemed to mind small deficiencies in standard middle-class arrangements, given the brilliant *mise-en-scène,* the good food, and the company.

Food

There were lots of memorable meals. Alan's affinity for food, and his friendship with Ally Anderson, who worked at the *Village Voice,* landed him the food-writing gig. He and co-conspirator Lale Armstrong adopted the pen name "FAT," and he wrote about himself in the third person. FAT took friends to restaurants, bakeries, ice cream shops, and souvlaki stands, and he wrote them into the piece. Once he strayed from edibles and reviewed a Russian steam bath on St. Mark's Place. The same drollness displayed in his designs cropped up in the FAT pieces: EIGHTH STREET, IN CASE YOU WEREN'T LOOKING LAST MONTH, HAS TURNED FROM SHOE CITY INTO CREAMTOWN. ONE NOW NEED WALK NO MORE THAN 30 YARDS FOR AN ICE CREAM HIT. ONE REASON FOR THIS SOCIO-GASTRONOMICAL PHENOMENON MAY BE THE RENTS. THEY ARE ASTRO-NOMICAL ON EIGHTH STREET, AND WHERE COULD YOU MAKE MORE PROFIT THAN FROM SELLING AIR? AND AIR IN SOME CASES CONSTI-TUTES AS MUCH AS 50 PERCENT OF ICE CREAM CONTENT . . . A FRIEND, WHOM WE SUSPECT SELLS CONES TO CARVEL, THINKS THEIR ICE CREAM IS THE BEST. WE DON'T. IT'S TOO ICY, NOT CREAMY ENOUGH, AND ONE

FLAVOR IN PARTICULAR GETS THE "MOST DISGUSTING TASTE SENSA-
TION EVER" RATING. A COMBINE OF EACH DAY'S LEFTOVER FLAVORS,
IT'S CALLED TREASURE ISLAND BUT IT TASTES MORE LIKE RIKER'S . . .
("EIGHTH STREET: WHAT'S THE SCOOP?")

I went along to gorge at Eileen's Special Cheesecake on Lafayette Street and to a huge feast at the newly opened Soho Charcuterie, where Alan's friends Jim and Colette Rossant lent their expert palates to a boisterous sampling of too many dishes. By contrast, we noticed the *Times'* John Canaday in the corner quietly concentrating on his meal. Once Alan persuaded his friend Serge, who ran Raoul's on Prince Street, to let him wait on tables and write about it. We decided this was too good an opportunity to pass up and booked a table for that evening. Alan's service was superb, especially attentive, up to the point that Dustin Hoffman came in and sat down across from us with a female companion. We were finally able to flag down Alan-the-waiter again much later, and he overcompensated with huge dessert portions.

Outside of New York, in places like Cincinnati or Louisville, Alan suffered withdrawal from New York food culture, though he enjoyed an occasional Big Mac. In his hometown, Savannah, however, we made the happy pilgrimage to Johnny Harris's for barbecue. We felt like insiders as we slid into one of the booths in the big circle and Alan was greeted warmly by black waiters in Eisenhower jackets who had been there since his childhood.

Our client couple in Savannah were well known, movers and shakers involved in business, politics, and real estate. He had a big white Jaguar and she had a huge white Cadillac, and we cut a swath as we drove around town or pulled up at one of the few night spots near the waterfront. Their project was an addition to and vivid redecoration of a gorgeous brick house, which served as our client's real estate office. We were careful to polish and leave undisturbed the superb original stairwell, but the colors, like our clients, were definitely not conservative, understated, or "historical" (unless your history includes the present). Alan's Savannah friends encouraged us to open an office there. I was enthusiastic, but I think Alan had mixed feelings about being back home. He was in his element plugged into the New York network.

A Savannah connection led us to a house in Columbia, South Carolina (pages 98–105). Alan had designed an ecstatically bright, patterned decorating project for one branch of the Tenenbaum family in Savannah (pages 52–55) and an apartment job for another Tenenbaum living in New York, so when Samuel Tenenbaum, who had opened a branch of the family steel business in Columbia, thought about building a house, he called the family architect.

For a variety of reasons, some of which I'm not sure of but will speculate about later, it became my project, though Alan contributed throughout and put the furnishings together. The client was a distant cousin of Alan's and the house is a distant cousin of the California Case Study Houses, interbred with a Manhattan loft. The client's business suggested that this could be the best opportunity one could ever have to design a steel-frame house. A massive perforated red wall is central to the idea of this house, and we decided that we should use a slightly cooler shade of red on the inside face to make it appear similar in incandescent light to the exterior in daylight. Alan's strategy was then to play off a whole world of greens against that dominant red element, but not let it look like Christmas. He had a rug made from a favorite photograph of tree branches, so that the floor seems to participate in the views visible out the windows. A dark blue-green metal staircase spirals to the upper level where a cool light green catwalk hangs off the wall.

Working out colors with Alan on this and other projects left a lasting impression on me. I'm not sure I could spell out the lessons: use lots of colors; work across color families; change hues, not just values; think about lighting color; work against a handsome ground; to thine own self be true.

The Tenenbaum House was beautifully photographed twice, once by Norman McGrath, propped and art directed by *House and Garden,* and again, more minimally, by Oberto Gili for *Architectural Record.* Alan secured art and objects with Elizabeth Sverbeyeff's help for the *House and Garden* shoot. He and I drove all the precious stuff down in a rented truck, stopping only to admire Monticello, and after the shoot our client liked the finishing touches so much that he bought them.

Fame

Most people connect Alan with his celebrity clientele: Bette Midler, Diane Keaton, Ellen Barkin, Joel Grey, Mandy Patinkin, Billy Joel and Christy Brinkley, et al. Those clients did create a buzz around the office, as well as among our contractors and suppliers. Alan liked to impersonate a flooring installer who had the opportunity to work for Joel Grey, whom he revered. "Believe me, Mr. Buchsbaum," Alan would repeat in his best Brooklynese, "This is really a thrill."

Alan also enjoyed those clients immensely. They could appreciate the flair and excitement of his work, artist to artist. The designs were personal, the result of their sensibilities and his. Bette's loft, for instance, was all Bette and Alan, notwithstanding organizing "pedestrian street" concepts or specific details contributed by others of us. Through this personal connection, friendships formed, so that it was not surprising to see a photograph in the *Daily News* of Diane Keaton running across the street after the theater with a bearded "unidentified companion" who happened to be her architect.

Among the celebrities, Bette Midler in particular made life interesting. One morning the answering machine, a relatively new device, which at that time we had not realized was a theatrical medium, yielded a lengthy, hilarious, Oscar-winning performance/message, which we saved on the tape for months. It topped even the most clever contemporary message efforts of Marty the Seltzer Man, who did a kind of Lawrence Welk bubble number from the seltzer factory. The raw space of Bette's loft was particularly stunning. My greatest hope when I first saw it was that the finished product would look almost as good as the before pictures; but Alan and Bette did better. I am still mesmerized by Oberto Gili's *House and Garden* shot of a Hudson River sunset out the windows behind the glistening sofa and gleaming floors (page 164–65).

Upstairs to Downstairs at Greene Street

It is hard to separate Alan's work from his personal style, and in fact the first loft on Greene Street made almost no physical separation between life and work. The drafting tables looked at the kitchen. Leaving the dishes undone or the bed unmade meant having a messy office. The efforts of the cleaning person, a young would-be actor who also worked for Susan Sontag, were critical. This was hardly corporate. We tried to imagine I. M. Pei wandering around in the drafting room/kitchen, and wondered if SOM's lawyer came in during the holidays to bake traditional fruitcake presents, as ours did.

After Louis Gancher and his nuts and bolts inventory cleared out of the first floor, we were able to build a separate mezzanine level there, which gave Alan greater privacy for his living quarters. The first-floor office was less dramatic than the third floor but more workable. We now had a large conference room, access to basement storage, and a kitchen under a classic Soho skylight in the back. Among the few mistakes in the cause of style was the all-flat-black bathroom—impossible to keep pristine in an office. The general feeling was looser than upstairs, which was more "fixed up" and glossy (all that free Mid-State tile) and had a more memorable overall image. Downstairs, Gancher's massive built-in scale was still in place, and operational, near the loading dock. Later, an auto seat bench (right), covered in sparkling vinyl like those installed by Alan and Davis Sprinkle in the nearby Moondance Diner, and a Jackelope (jack rabbit as antelope) head from Oklahoma on the wall added to the eclectic flavor. Harry Snare and Irene Delusion, Alan's cats, roamed desks and drooled on drawings. They had seats dedicated in their names in the first Film Forum cinema, as did Diane Keaton's cat Buster.

Japanese Tudor

Not too long after we moved downstairs in the late seventies Lale Armstrong joined our partnership, bringing along some real live projects and several staff people. She and others helped execute furnishings for a house that Mark Simon and Charles Moore were designing in Camotop (Potomac spelled backwards), Maryland (pages 94–95). In addition to custom furniture they came up with a wonderful family of custom wallpapers, "Dot's Trellis," which was screened (hence the dots), enlarged, and abstracted from a William Morris trellis paper—sort of Arts and Crafts Lichtenstein. Various screened overlays were added to the basic trellis pattern as one moved around the house, building in a meaningful progression, which I can't remember. I never saw the house, but Charles Moore said it was "Japanese Tudor."

The project was Alan's closest brush with Postmodernism, and aided and abetted by Moore and Simon he kept a playful edge. A glass coffee-table top was supported by a model of Michelangelo's Laurentian Library staircase. The television was supposed to be housed in a cabinet tower with a Robert Adam cutout face frame. This media high-rise, a kind of mini-AT&T, was reported in a story on Alan to have been "too much" for the client. Some of us wondered if such a thing were possible. It was also true that the complete unit with finial was simply too tall for the soffited corner for which it was intended. As a result, it stood for a while near our first-floor office entrance, sounding yet another post-tech stylistic note until it was sent out on consignment.

Vocabularies

There was usually something cooking on Alan's drafting board, if not a furniture plan (below) then a large-scale wall elevation in soft pencil on yellow tracing paper. He never got so busy or businesslike that his desk was clear or his hands free. Sometimes it was hard to tell which project was on the board, because he kept working in the same themes, rearranging elements, introducing favorite objects. He was loose and flexible in his planning, and the final products took a very different character. But it was always clearly his work, not just a sympathetic response to a context. Alan may have had an allergy to "isms" or labels, but he did employ a vocabulary, one that changed but was still identifiable. Working with a vocabulary also made it possible to build without enormously elaborate contract documents. We knew that the Cavallacis in their Queens marble yard could follow the apparently natural jagged edge carefully traced out for the stone counter or table, and that we could re-dimension the welded-steel wall bracket that supported the last stone counter. Bette Midler's dining table had clear antecedents in the table we designed for Walter Bernstein, and so on. Alan harvested ideas he liked, often improving and manipulating them to suit his current projects, taking X-leg drafting tables I had designed for the office, for example, and squashing  them so they would work beautifully as coffee tables in Diane Keaton's apartment (overleaf). He also attempted to make sure publications appropriately credited his co-workers and collaborators, who included Lale Armstrong, Corey Delany, Howard Korenstein, Marc L'Italien, German Martinez, Davis Sprinkle, and me.

Spacemaking/Playmaking

When there were occasional projects with an out-doors, Alan's attention gravitated inside. I was some-what surprised at this division of labor, but I did the few additions and house projects that came our way, including interiors when Alan was otherwise occu-pied. Not that there was an iron curtain; ideas moved back and forth as in any collaboration. I can only speculate at the reasons for Alan's interior focus. He may have felt that exterior materials were generally too drab or shaped by public requirements, though the signage at the Moondance Diner (pages 140–41) suggests he could bring his inventive, irreverent powers to bear outdoors as well as indoors. No doubt I moved eagerly to get my hands on projects that seemed like real *buildings,* but I think Alan ceded ground because his muse was more Magritte than Piranesi. The realm he preferred and was most capable in was a kind of imaginative theater. It started with the transformation of a given surround and required an invented population of objects, some-times with a narrative or narrative fragment (as in his Casa Tile installa-tions) but usually animated by the clients and arranged for their com-fort. This is a scenographic talent, working magic with arresting colors and lighting, investing wit in our domestic artifacts, containers, appli-ances, and enclosures; as I experienced it, Alan's gift was not primarily for the construction of three-dimensional volumes or spaces. When we worked together in this way Alan did make suggestions and push for certain outcomes. An offhanded comment broke up a color logjam as I was designing the first Film Forum cinema, for example, and he pro-moted my concept for the Tenenbaum House in South Carolina. But he chomped at the bit until he could start drawing a furnishing plan.

The Domestic Collage

The furnishing plans were beautiful and stylized. Watching Alan, I start-ed to do facsimiles, even cultivating the characteristic, sometimes illegi-ble, soft-pencil script labels. Shadows made chairs, tables, sinks, and tubs pop. Shadow template lettering brought titles into the composition. Mix-and-match flooring patterns provided a ground for the collage: stripes (wood or tile), checkerboards or grids (usually tile), and various textures for carpet. Offbeat penciled color combinations reaching across color families gave areas strength or made tiny details visible; all of this, as always, was laid down on paper in the softest possible lead, not too sharp. Alan had a confident, fluid hand that made these diagrams flow, even through it occasionally contributed to a sense of glib contrivance. The hand was evident, pushing, pulling, skewing, but still relaxed. However modest the component—toilet, sink, countertop—it took on another life beyond its mundane purpose, artfully welded into an idiosyncratic composition.

This technique of patterned collage was at the heart of Alan's way of working. There was no apparent theoretical rigor to it, but more a restless intuitive search for interest, pattern, surprise, drama, a search for a casual, comfortable order. As the seventies gave way to the more complicated eighties, the comprehensive geometries in Alan's work gave way to (carefully) jousting shards and fragments, full of kinks and rough edges and loose "unfits." Stepped patterns were a favorite of Alan's; as time went on he used them more frequently as design molecules bouncing among a set of other thoughtfully dissimilar events and less frequently as an organizing device. A stepping pattern, for example, might find itself married to a curved surface, as happened in Bette Midler's (right) and Alan's lofts. The overall misfit was a calculated way of improving the fit to interesting, complicated clients, not to mention to an interesting, complicated designer. Alan's physics were those of quarks and spin and strangeness, not those of planets moving majestically through ether (a cosmology that seems to underlie one strand of Modernism).

What's Wrong with these Pictures?

I sometimes felt a need to provide some of that ether, to tie all the interesting events together and perhaps space them out a little, to provide some silence as datum. This resistance may arise from the cultural momentum of cool, rational Modernism, fighting progress. If I were to develop this intuition into a criticism, I would start with an appreciation of Alan's mastery of the vignette. He could make metaphors, push disparate things together, see striking combinations of shape and color. This way of working was friendly to the camera; the natural affinity between shelter journalism and Alan's work was not just the result of his conviviality or genius for public relations. The work had merit; it was novel, newsworthy, and especially photogenic. It was no accident that the glass-block wall and tiled sleeping area of his third-floor loft were used as the backdrop for a particularly distracting lingerie shoot one week, or that Tommy Lee Jones and Faye Dunaway were around at another time shooting *The Eyes of Laura Mars* in Rosalind Krauss's loft and the stairwell. The designs worked marvelously as sets, since a certain kind of "picturesqueness," in the most positive sense of the term, was part of their conception.

If one goes out on enough limbs some will bend and some will break. The fact that some of Alan's work now looks dated, like the early super-graphics (right) or some of the slick apartments, is not an indictment. Interior designs have a certain life; they are the venues for fashion, for people's lives, for occasional brilliantly lightweight "camping out" as opposed to building for all time. His work faltered when the stunning vignette was hard to live with over time, when there were too many inventive ideas vying for attention, when the overall spatial idea was weakened or displaced by local interest, or when inspired iconoclasm decayed into self-indulgence. As time went on there seemed to be fewer one-liners, and a sense of increasing assurance suggested that even better work was ahead when he died.

Nonsummary

Alan would have viewed homages and reprises like the present one with suspicion (there is no way to fight back); his impulse was defamatory and away from formality. He seemed to like the (minor) spotlight well enough, nevertheless, so that he would also have been somewhat pleased. Whatever else he was or was not, whatever other walls he built, he kept a clear channel to his work. That work showed a strong personal stamp, fearless in its own way, unafraid of color, quirkiness, crankiness, or even triviality at times, full of evidence of characteristic dispositions, preferences, and moods. Alan's approach was not couched in theoretical but in immediate and personal terms, fashionable in an off-the-mark sense, mightily concerned about the impression but intent on flying off, like the eagles on his letterhead, away from "good taste." It may be that part of what we still find compelling is this direct connection—the humanity that for better or for worse shows directly through the work. Our experience of codified repetition, minimalism that erases any imprints, or abstract manic assemblages has left some of us with an appetite for his kind of home cooking.

ALAN BUCHSBAUM
& DESIGN COALITION

BARROON

1967

design   Alan Buchsbaum and Kazz Morimoto
production   Beylerian
photography   courtesy George Beylerian
text   Frederic Schwartz

Described as "punchy puffs of air-filled vinyl that can tumble with children or hold a small TV," the Japanese "Barroon," an inflatable vinyl hassock in shiny white, red, or black, was a decorating bargain at only $5.00. This durable twenty-inch-diameter vinyl air-stool that doubled as a toy was both functional and light-hearted. The hassock was exhibited in the show "High Styles: Eight Decades of Vanguard Design" at the Whitney Museum of American Art in 1985.

PAPER POPPY

New York, New York
1968

design   Design Coalition: Alan Buchsbaum assisted by Irene Grabowich
photography   Peter Hujar
text   Frederic Schwartz

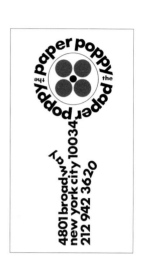

Selling greeting cards, paperbacks, and psychedelic gifts, this shop attracted attention to its out-of-the-way Upper Broadway location with its bold, mannerist super-graphics. The design of red and black bands in porcelain-enameled steel panels ran unfinished into brick walls and windows. The same design was continued inside, where fluid linear graphics reinforced the circulation. The striped bands ended in a flourish over the cash register. Clusters of red and purple lights repeating the store logo were also found on the walls, inlaid on the vinyl asbestos floor, and printed on the stationery and shopping bags. For the window display Buchsbaum used an elegant German display system of glass panels with plastic connectors.

METAMORPHOSIS

Great Neck, New York
1969

design	Design Coalition: Alan Buchsbaum
photography	Norman McGrath
text	Frederic Schwartz

Buchsbaum designed Metamorphosis, a women's beauty salon and men's clothing store in the Long Island suburbs, as an inhabitable work of Pop Art, a full-scale fantasy of mod colors, finishes, forms, and super-graphics. The exterior, faced with one-foot strips of red porcelain-enameled steel, featured glass windows and two doors with giant-scaled human profiles, one for each shop.

The curving interior wall that separated the store from the salon was painted in ten shades of lipstick pink and one shade of eye-shadow blue; the "VIP" room, or pedicure area, sported floor-to-ceiling horizontal stripes in a full spectrum of colors. Cabinets in white laminate, chairs in shiny white vinyl, and a white tile floor with inlaid bands of pink exaggerated the entry and seating area.

Beneath the distracting surfaces and sensations, a rational plan organized the salon's multi-staged program. Metamorphosis was an efficient workplace and highly stylized commercial architecture. The owner noted, "People feel young when they're here, and I know that the architect's design will be modern for many years to come."

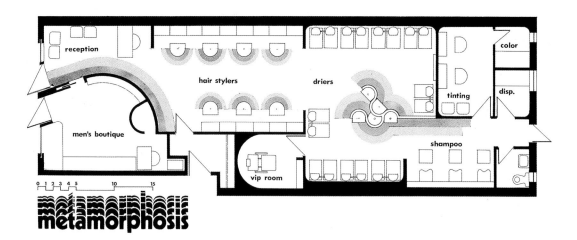

WE USED PINK PREDOMINANTLY TO SHOW THAT IT WAS POSSIBLE TO TAKE SOME-
THING OBVIOUS, EVEN KITSCH, AND GIVE IT AN ENTIRELY NEW FEELING.

CADO SHOWROOM

Los Angeles, California
1969

design	Design Coalition: Alan Buchsbaum
lighting consultants	Jules Fisher and Paul Marantz
photography	Robert Wortham
text	Frederic Schwartz

The design of the ceiling and lighting is paramount in this 3,000-square-foot housewares showroom. The company's name is painted on the acoustic-tile ceiling in enormous bold red super-graphics. Conventional two-by-four-foot fluorescent fixtures with various pendant-mounted tracks and single bare lamps, all in a riotous juxtaposition, are attached to the ceiling tiles following their own patterns, rhythms, and logic. "Cubex" storage units are highlighted by lamps strung from the white path between the red lines of the overhead letters; two feet below the ceiling, the lamps provide the illusion of a sparkling plane.

Multi-colored, see-through fabric screens (Mira-X voiles) wire-hung from the ceiling define display areas and furniture settings. Buchsbaum used standard acoustic tile in an unconventional way, running the pattern diagonal to the building walls. At the edge, the tiles zigzag and are held back from the wall so that the space of the showroom stands apart from its enclosure. Thus the white ceiling visually "floats" in the same shadowy surround that sets off the strategically spotlit merchandise.

I LIKE THE AESTHETIC OF L.A. BETTER THAN NEW YORK. I THINK THAT NEW YORK IS A LITTLE BIT UPTIGHT AND I'M NOT VERY FOND OF POSTMODERNISM AND I'M NOT FOND OF DESIGN IN A HISTORICAL CONTEXT. I THINK IT'S MORE INTERESTING TO BE ONE OF THOSE PEOPLE WHO ARE LUCKY ENOUGH TO INVENT SOMETHING AS OPPOSED TO SOMEONE WHO TAKES SOMETHING AND REFINES IT AND RE-CREATES IT.

GERBER HOUSE

Chappaqua, New York
1969

design	Design Coalition: Alan Buchsbaum and Howard Korenstein
photography	Norman McGrath
text	Design Coalition

The design for this 3,000-square-foot, cubic, classic, late-sixties house developed from the strong relationship between the site, the sun, and the family's budget-conscious program. The variety of window sizes, placements, and shapes were selected to frame specific views and, according to Buchsbaum, BY THE RELAXED THEORY THAT SOME ARE FOR FUNCTION, AND SOME ARE FOR FUN. Mrs. Gerber said, "It's all a great success because I feel as if I am on a permanent vacation, constantly bathing in sunshine." Design Coalition described the house in an AIA Awards application:

THE PROGRAM CONSISTS OF LIVING ROOM, DINING ROOM, KITCHEN, PLAYROOM, THREE CHILDREN'S BEDROOMS, MASTER BEDROOM SUITE, MAID'S BEDROOM, INDOOR SWIMMING POOL, AND SAUNA. THE HOUSE IS DIVIDED INTO THREE FUNCTIONAL AREAS ON THREE LEVELS—SWIMMING POOL AND SERVICE, LIVING, AND SLEEPING. THE STACKING OF THE HOUSE SAVED ON THE COST OF CONSTRUCTION AND GAVE THE FEELING OF LIVING IN THE TREES. ALTHOUGH BOUNTIFUL IN ACREAGE, THE STEEP AND ROCKY SITE WAS LIMITED IN TERMS OF BUILDABLE AREA. THE VIEW IS OF A HEAVILY WOODED VALLEY. TO PROVIDE AS MUCH SUN AS POSSIBLE IN THE POOL AND LIVING AREAS, THE HOUSE FACES SOUTHWEST. TO INCREASE THE DRAMA OF THE HOUSE, IT IS CANTILEVERED OVER THE ROCKY SLOPE. THIS ALSO SITUATES THE OUTDOOR DECKS AND LIVING AREAS ON A LEVEL WITH THE LEAF MASSES OF THE TREES AND ENHANCES THE VIEW DOWN INTO THE VALLEY. THE FLAT ENTRY FACADE SUGGESTS SOMETHING SPECIAL INSIDE AND FEATURES A BRIGHT RED LACQUERED DOOR WITH AN ASYMMETRICAL COMPOSITION OF PORTHOLE WINDOWS TO THE LEFT AND SLIGHTLY OFF-SHIFTING VERTICAL WINDOWS ABOVE. THE CHILDREN'S BEDROOMS ARE CANTILEVERED OVER THE LIVING ROOM WALLS, DEFINING THE THIRD LEVEL AND PROVIDING SUN PROTECTION FOR THE LIVING ROOM AND UPPER DECK DURING THE SUMMER MONTHS. A HOLE CUT OUT OF THE MAIN FLOOR VISUALLY INTEGRATES THE LIVING AND POOL AREAS. THE INTERIOR GLASS WALL AROUND THE OPENING PROVIDES TEMPERATURE AND HUMIDITY SEPARATION. THE MAJOR LIVING SPACES AND THE BATHROOMS ARE PAVED WITH DARK BROWN QUARRY TILE, AND THE PLAYROOM HAS WHITE VINYL ASBESTOS TILE. ALL OTHER AREAS HAVE OAK STRIP FLOORING. THE INTERIORS ARE SHEETROCK PAINTED WITH WHITE SEMIGLOSS PAINT. IN SPECIAL ROOMS THERE ARE BANDS OF BRIGHT COLOR. FOR EXAMPLE, IN THE PLAYROOM, TWO ORANGE BANDS DELINEATE A SPACE WHERE THE CHILDREN MAY DRAW ON THE WALL; IN THE POOL ROOM, A MURAL OF WAVES IN SEVERAL SHADES OF BLUE AND GREEN IS BALANCED BY GIANT, POP ART, ORANGE AND LEMON LIFESAVER SHAPES; THE KITCHEN PASS-THROUGH IS DELINEATED IN BOLD YELLOW AND RED RACING STRIPES; AND THE STAIRWELL CARRIES THE RED, ORANGE, AND BUFF COLORS THROUGHOUT. THE LIGHTS AND WHITE PLASTIC FURNITURE ARE FROM ITALY.

ANYBODY CAN MAKE A CUBE; BUT HOW DO YOU MAKE IT INTERESTING?

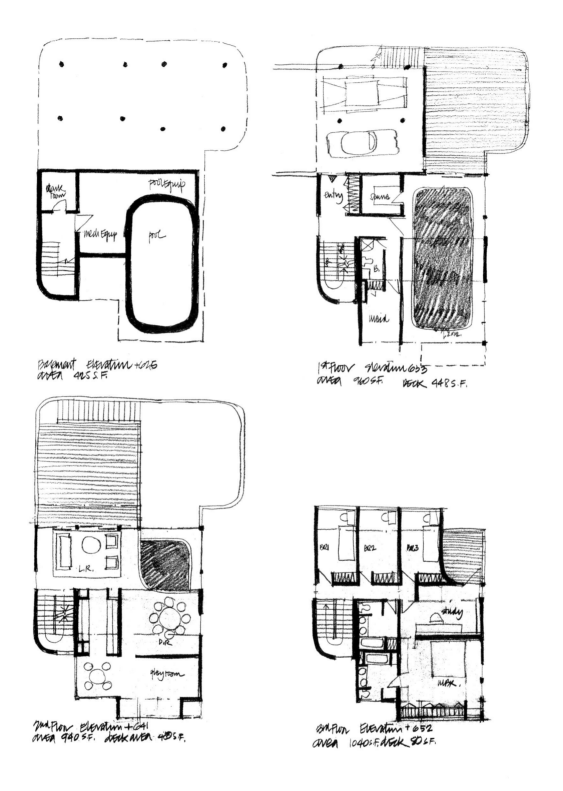

Basement Elevation +626
area 425 S.F.

1st Floor Elevation 633
area 960 S.F.   Deck 448 S.F.

2nd Floor Elevation +641
area 940 S.F. deck area 40 S.F.

3rd Floor Elevation +652
area 1040 S.F. deck 80 S.F.

ROSENBERG HOUSE

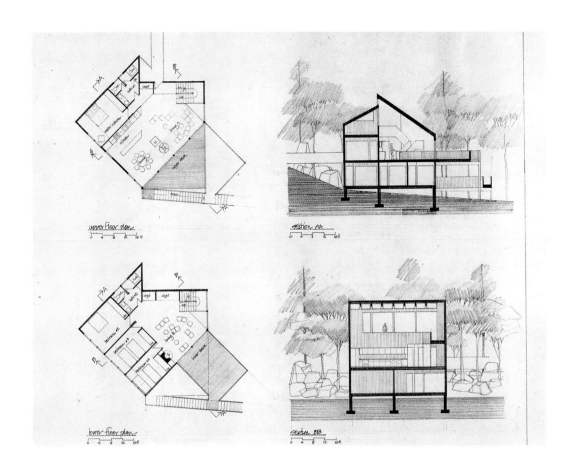

upper floor plan

section AA

lower floor plan

section BB

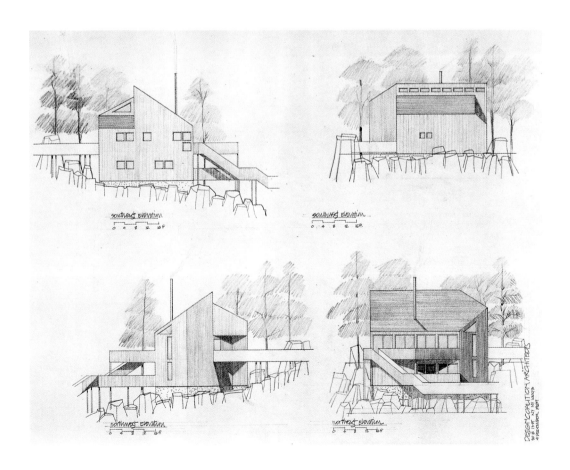

southeast elevation

southwest elevation

northwest elevation

northeast elevation

ROSENBERG HOUSE

Rome, Maine
1969

design   Design Coalition: Alan Buchsbaum and Howard Korenstein
photography   Norman McGrath
text   Frederic Schwartz

The irregular form of this 2,750-square-foot vacation home developed from distortions in the simple plan to accommodate views, site, and program. Located on the edge of a lake, the house was built entirely of wood and shaped to fit the sloping terrain. Each window was placed to ensure maximum sunlight and to frame views.

Buchsbaum and Korenstein designed three separate zones as well as generous communal space with bridges and stairs branching off from the different levels to accommodate indoor and outdoor, year-round use by a family of three generations. Interior elements were reduced to a minimum in accordance with the owners' desire to "rough it in comfort."

SIMPLICITY WAS THE KEYNOTE FOR THE DINING ROOM. THE WALLS AND TABLE ARE MADE OF KNOTTY PINE, WHICH GIVES THE ROOM AN OVERALL COHESIVE LOOK AND FEEL. MOST OF THE DRAMA COMES FROM THE USE OF TRACK LIGHTING AND JUST A TOUCH OF RED IN THE CHAIRS. BECAUSE KNOTTY PINE IS PLENTIFUL IN MAINE, AND THUS INEXPENSIVE, IT WAS A PARTICULARLY GOOD WOOD TO USE. USING WOOD INDIGENOUS TO A PARTICULAR LOCALE IS USUALLY A GOOD MONEY-SAVING IDEA.

HAAS APARTMENT

New York, New York
1973

design	Design Coalition: Alan Buchsbaum and Howard Korenstein
photography	Norman McGrath
text	Frederic Schwartz

In this Manhattan apartment, Buchsbaum designed an oak wall unit that is at once desk, bar, media center, and bookshelves, housing the television, stereo, a small refrigerator, and wine storage. Additionally, the unit folds back as a moveable wall. Closed, it conceals a guest room; opened, it reveals an extra seating area.

The wall unit's clean rectilinear geometry is accented by an upside-down and slightly twisted ziggurat of glassware storage with angles inspired by the floorboards. The mirrored countertop above the refrigerator contrasts with the matte oak, contributing an interesting off-note.

Small apartments should inspire designers to find particularly creative solutions. The bold use of color to delineate function, form, and structure, the challenge of clever space planning for all programs, and the design of multifunction wall units were constant preoccupations throughout Buchsbaum's career.

I STILL HEAR MY COLLEAGUES SAY THAT THEY WISH MANUFACTURERS OF BUILDING MATERIALS AND HOME FURNISHINGS—PLASTIC LAMINATE, CERAMIC TILE, TOWELS, SHOWER CURTAINS—WOULD ARRANGE TO HAVE THEIR PRODUCTS COLOR COORDINATE. I CAN'T THINK OF A MORE INFINITELY BORING IDEA. CAN YOU IMAGINE GOING INTO A FOREST THAT HAS LEAVES ALL ONE COLOR? SOLID AVOCADO? HARVEST GOLD?

TENENBAUM INTERIORS

Savannah, Georgia
1972

design   Alan Buchsbaum with Gunn & Meyerhoff
photography   Bill Maris
text   Susan Grant Lewin, "Out of Yesterday"

Born in Savannah, Buchsbaum returned in 1972 to collaborate on the interior design of a gracious nineteenth-century mansion. Susan Grant Lewin, architecture editor of *House Beautiful,* lavishly published the interiors, which accommodated a mixture of cultural and stylistic influences—antiques, fine art, and super-graphics:

"Every color scheme in the 6,400-square-foot townhouse, begins with either beige, red, or blue (the colors of the Marimekko entry hall fabric). All is low-key and underplayed in the soft beige living and dining rooms. In the study red takes over and becomes the dominant color of the house.

"Red arrows, flowers, bull's eyes, chevrons, and other assorted abstractions and geometrics run riot in the children's rooms. Touches of blue, green, yellow, pink, and white are thrown in for good measure."

ALTHOUGH WE DEFINITELY EMPHASIZED GRAPHICS, COLOR, TEXTURE, AND PATTERN, OUR OBJECTIVE WAS TO ACCENTUATE THE ARCHITECTURE OF THE HOUSE, NOT TO HIDE IT. IT WAS THIS THINKING THAT LED US TO USE A DARK STAIN FOR THE ORIGINAL WOODWORK TRIM IN THE INTERCONNECTING LIVING AND DINING ROOMS. THE DARK WOODWORK IN ESSENCE BECOMES AN OUTLINE FOR THE FORMS OF THE TWO ROOMS. SINCE ALL THE CHILDREN'S ROOMS ARE CONNECTED, I THOUGHT IT WOULD BE FUN TO EMPHASIZE THIS RELATIONSHIP BY KEEPING THE COLORS SIMILAR BUT PLAYING THE DIFFERENTLY SCALED PATTERNS AGAINST EACH OTHER. IT'S ALL AN EXERCISE IN SCALE, COLOR, AND PATTERN COMBINATION.

LEWIN APARTMENT

New York, New York
1972

design   Alan Buchsbaum assisted by Dan Boscescu
photography   Bill Maris
text   Susan Grant Lewin

Working with Alan on my own apartment, I had the privilege of observing his design process up close. The place he wanted to begin was my son Adam's room. The concept behind the design was measurement. The large room became a brilliant juxtaposition of the metric system and the American system of feet and inches. In jolting primaries, Alan circled the room with rulers marking the varying dimensions. Near the door he created a place to measure the children's growth: Adam was still a baby so Alan held him up to the wall and traced his amorphous shape; Jeanne was then about six so Alan silhouetted her against the wall; and Gaby was only an idea but her presence was felt, so a small shape was created for her. Large geometric toy shapes took precedence over furniture. But most important were the circular rugs that Alan designed in parrot green, red, white, blue, and yellow. Alan asked me to go to Chinatown to get a giant red canvas fish, which I did. At this point he concluded, the room "finished."

Big, bold, and colorful jolts of red permeated the rest of the apartment and gave life to the very white walls in the kitchen, living room, bedroom, even the bathroom. Alan selected shades of bright green wool for the foam-furniture covers, brilliant Marimekko textiles, and a Danese red-apple wall hanging. In the dining area he selected from Acerbis a white table with a bright orange extension, which still serves us well. When we photographed the room for *House Beautiful,* Alan carried through with the styling, insisting on a rubber tree for the living room that he selected himself.

3M

4M

5M

6M

10

20

10

15

20

12

15

18

21

14

16

18

20

12

10

FOAM FURNITURE
1972

design   Alan Buchsbaum
photography   Bill Maris
text   Susan Grant Lewin

Whenever possible, Alan wanted to design furniture.
For my apartment, he had the idea of doing a varia-
tion on the furniture Matta had designed for Knoll.
We drove out to a foam-rubber factory in Huntington,
Long Island. Once there, Alan became fascinated by
the various densities of foam and decided to combine several types in one piece with brightly colored
stretch-fabric coverings.

overleaf

BATHROOM
1971

design   Alan Buchsbaum
photography   Wesley Balz
text   Frederic Schwartz

Buchsbaum's objective, for a *House Beautiful* story,
was to rethink the traditional bathroom. In so doing,
he not only found space for additional fixtures but
also intimated new ways for the body to be in the
bathroom.

In separating a grooming anteroom from the rest of
the bathroom, Buchsbaum created a much-appreci-
ated dry space for make-up and mirrors. In the
"wet" room, he exploded the normally rectilinear
composition of fixtures by projecting the toilet,
bidet, and tub off the plumbing core at varying
angles. In contrast, a circular sink floated indepen-
dently, and the shower platform, accessed by a
short stair, efficiently took up the residual space
behind the tub.

Buchsbaum used a bold and vibrant palette of primary yellow, bright red, and lime green in the
super-graphics style to reinforce his design of the
new bathroom.

HERE COMES TOMORROW
1973

design　　　　　Design Coalition: Alan Buchsbaum and Howard Korenstein
photography　　　　　　　　　　　　　　　　Bill Maris
text　　　　　　　　　　　　　　　　Frederic Schwartz

Buchsbaum and Korenstein designed three giant, bright red, suitcase-like furniture modules for "Here Comes Tomorrow," an exhibit sponsored by Owens-Corning Fiberglas first shown in Manhattan and then nationally. The modules opened into a dining area; a fold-out sleeping area; and a living and entertainment unit with a communications and media wall (two televisions, stereo, headphones, tape deck, speakers), a plant area, a mini-bar, and storage space. These modules created a completely furnished, multipurpose, twenty-four-hour environment. They were mounted on casters for practicality and to reflect the increasing mobility of the American family.

LLOYDS APARTMENT

New York, New York
1972

design   Design Coalition: Alan Buchsbaum and Howard Korenstein
photography   Norman McGrath
text   Alan Buchsbaum

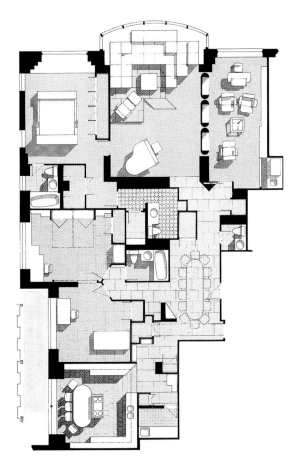

THE OWNER ASKED US TO DESIGN AN APARTMENT TO ACCOMMODATE HIM, HIS WIFE, AND THEIR TWO CHILDREN IN A COOPERATIVE BUILDING ON FIFTH AVENUE FACING CENTRAL PARK. THE ORIGINAL APARTMENT, WHILE HAVING SUFFICIENT SPACE, WAS UNSUITED TO THE DEMANDS OF THE NEW OWNERS' LIFESTYLE. OUR CLIENTS WANTED A GENEROUS LIVING ROOM AND STUDY, AN ADDITIONAL BATHROOM, AND PRIVACY FROM THE CHILDREN'S AREAS. THEY DID NOT NEED THE EXISTING MAID'S ROOM AND BATH, FORMAL DINING ROOM, AND SEPARATE SERVICE CORRIDOR. TO CONVERT THE APARTMENT TO THE NEW REQUIREMENTS, MORE THAN HALF OF THE WALLS WERE REMOVED. THE KITCHEN WAS ENLARGED, INCORPORATING THE MAID'S AREA AND SERVICE CORRIDOR, TO PROVIDE ENOUGH SPACE FOR A TABLE FOR FOOD PREPARATION AND DINING. A NEW BATHROOM WAS CREATED OUT OF STORAGE SPACE. LONG CORRIDORS WERE REMOVED AND MORE ARCHITECTURAL PASSAGES AND STORAGE AREAS WERE CREATED IN THEIR PLACE. THE CHILDREN WERE GIVEN THEIR OWN MULTIFUNCTION ENVIRONMENT WITH HIDE-AWAY BEDS AND BRIGHTLY COLORED FURNISHINGS. THE KITCHEN HAS CABINETS OF BIRCH AND ENGLISH OAK, AND ITS FLOOR AND WALLS ARE FINISHED WITH MEXICAN CHOCOLATE-BROWN TILES. THE FLOORS OF THE OTHER LIVING AND SLEEPING AREAS ARE COVERED WITH EITHER DARK BROWN MARBLE OR CARPET.

THE WALL BETWEEN THE LIVING ROOM AND THE STUDY WAS
REPLACED WITH THREE HIGH-GLOSS, WHITE-LACQUERED,
REVOLVING STORAGE/ART DISPLAY/SPEAKER CABINETS,
WHICH ALTER THE SPATIAL RELATIONSHIPS OF THE TWO
ROOMS AT OUR CLIENTS' WHIM. THE FURNISHINGS WERE
ENLARGED AND CONSOLIDATED BOTH TO SIMPLIFY AND TO
INCREASE THE APPARENT SPATIAL IMAGE OF THESE
ROOMS. A RAISED SEATING PLATFORM IN THE LIVING
ROOM ACCENTUATES THE CENTRAL PARK VIEW. ALL COL-
ORS WERE KEPT WITHIN TONES OF BROWN WITH THE
EXCEPTION OF THE BOOKCASE/BAR IN THE STUDY, WHICH
IS LACQUERED IN HIGH-GLOSS BRIGHT GREEN.

COHEN INTERIORS

Kendall, Florida
1973

design	Design Coalition: Alan Buchsbaum and Howard Korenstein
photography	Bill Maris
text	Frederic Schwartz

Three storage units double as space dividers in this modern, open-plan Florida house. Because of their size, the laminate-clad units were constructed in two parts and joined by horizontal bands of stainless steel. The paired units accommodate stereo equipment in one and a desk in the other. Set on rotating ball-bearings, they also turn to close off a guest bedroom/study from the living area. The single unit is a dry bar with storage for glassware, wine, and liquor; it can be moved to divide the living and dining areas.

12 GREENE STREET LOFTS

Alan Buchsbaum for *Gran Bazaar*

12 GREENE STREET, LOCATED IN HISTORIC SOHO, IS A LOFT BUILDING THAT WAS ORIGINALLY A CORD FACTORY. BUILT IN 1868 BY AN ARCHITECT NAMED RICHARD SNOOK, THE FACADE IS CAST IRON AND THE STRUCTURE IS HEAVY TIMBER. THE FRONT HALF OF THE BUILDING HAS NO COLUMNS; THE BACK HALF DOES. I ASSUME THAT THE BACK PART WAS USED FOR STORAGE. THE BUILDING IMMEDIATELY TO THE SOUTH IS THE TWIN OF THIS ONE AND WAS PROBABLY CONNECTED ON THE GROUND LEVEL.

IN 1976, I RENOVATED THE THIRD FLOOR FOR MY HOME AND OFFICE AND THE SECOND FLOOR FOR ROSALIND KRAUSS. BOB MORRIS FIXED UP THE FIFTH FLOOR FOR HIS USE AS AN ARTIST'S STUDIO. ROSALIND USED HER FLOOR AS AN OFFICE WHERE SHE EDITED *OCTOBER* AND AS LIVING SPACE. THE PLAN OF THIS FLOOR IS MORE FORMAL THAN THE OTHERS AND I THINK MORE ELEGANT. EACH FLOOR HAS A DIFFERENT CEILING HEIGHT AND A DIFFERENT USE, WHICH PARTIALLY EXPLAINS WHY THE DESIGNS ARE DIFFERENT. IN THE PLANS OF BOTH THE FIRST AND THIRD FLOORS, THE FEELING IS MORE INFORMAL AND THE DESIGN IS MEANT TO LOOK MORE ACCIDENTAL.

I'M AFRAID I HAVE NO STRICT RULES THAT GUIDE MY DESIGN. IF ANYTHING, YOU MIGHT CALL ME A PRAGMATIST. IN RENOVATING LOFT SPACES I FIND THAT THE VOLUMES AND WALL AREAS

ARE SO LARGE THAT TO FINISH THEM WITH NEW CONSTRUCTION WOULD BE PROHIBITIVELY EXPENSIVE. SO INSTEAD I FIND PLEASURE IN SEEING THE ROUGH QUALITY OF THE EXISTING CONSTRUCTION CONTRASTED WITH SHINY NEW MATERIALS.

THIS IS EVIDENT IN THE THIRD FLOOR, WHERE THE TILE MEETS THE WOODEN STRUCTURE OF THE BUILDING, AND IN THE FIRST FLOOR, WHERE EVEN THE NEW CON-STRUCTION WAS LEFT UNFIN-ISHED IN PLACES TO CONTRAST WITH THE FINISHED PARTS —FOR EXAMPLE, THE BATH-AREA CEILING, WHERE THE NEW WOOD JOISTS ARE LEFT EXPOSED AND A PATCH OF BRICK IS LEFT BARE BY THE AIR CONDITIONER.

THE FIRST FLOOR, WHICH WAS THE LAST FLOOR TO BE BUILT, INDICATES AN INTER-EST I NOW HAVE WITH COLOR. EACH COLOR IS MEANT TO BE "OUT OF SYNC" WITH THE OTHERS. THERE ARE GREENS TOGETHER THAT HAVE YELLOW AND BLUE HUES, GRAYS THAT ARE WARM AND COOL NEXT TO EACH OTHER. NO WALL IS PAINTED THE SAME COLOR.

I THINK I'VE TALKED ENOUGH. I DON'T LIKE TO SPEAK ABOUT MY DESIGN; I WOULD PREFER TO READ YOUR REACTION TO IT.

KRAUSS LOFT

New York, New York
1976

design	Alan Buchsbaum
photography	Norman McGrath
text	Rosalind Krauss

Several years after the completion of this loft, the art critic Robert Hughes entered it, looked around, and said, "The Bauhaus lives!" And indeed, in this unadorned space the effect is entirely constructed from the intersection of the envelope formed by the long, continuous planes of gleaming floor and luminous pressed-tin ceiling, stretching ninety feet from one bank of windows to the other, with the block of the "utilities" area topped by the mezzanine that crosses this envelope on an angle.

White planes, white pilotis, white tile, white cabinets, no ornament: nothing is going on in this interior except its parti, by which the "idea" of loft-as-open-space is tenaciously maintained. It is only in the detailing that one feels the ironic twists of Buchsbaum's own playfulness: the bathtub sunk into the plane of the floor repeated by the exposed bowl of the sink sunk into the floating marble plane of the counter; the mattress plane of the bed floating above the dining area's ceiling, which rises to support it above the plane of the mezzanine's floor. Subtle shifts in level to articulate the functions of this simple crossed axis are almost all that Buchsbaum allowed himself in this space that he made as a concession to the taste of a friend.

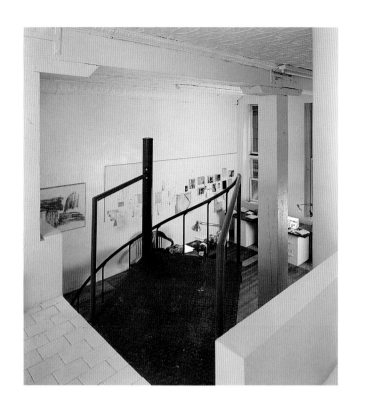

BUCHSBAUM LOFT 1

New York, New York
1976

design	Design Coalition: Alan Buchsbaum with Stephen Tilly
photography	Norman McGrath
text	Norma Skurka, "Fixturing Up a Loft"

Buchsbaum transformed a raw manufacturing space at 12 Greene Street into his own highly stylized live-work loft. His early use of off-the-shelf and high- and low-tech materials such as glass block, Metro shelving, commercial tile, restaurant equipment, and factory lighting was trendsetting in the development of loft design. Buchsbaum's free-flowing open plan combined functional areas defined by materials, lighting, and offbeat furniture groupings with an occasional conventional room for work or guests. The loft included a carpeted "dining pit" and a curving glass-block wall outlined by blue airport runway lights. In 1977 Norma Skurka wrote the following detailed description for the *New York Times Magazine:*

THE LAMPS FOR THE KITCHEN COST ABOUT $21.00 APIECE. IT'S ALMOST IMPOSSIBLE TO FIND A WELL-DESIGNED HANGING LAMP FOR THAT PRICE IN A RETAIL STORE. THESE LIGHTS ARE RUGGED AND DURABLE. CONSIDERATIONS OF TASTE AND AESTHETICS PLAYED NO PART IN THEIR DESIGN.

PLEASE DON'T PIN ANY LABEL ON MY WORK. I HAVE NO PHILOSOPHY TO
SPEAK OF, THERE'S NO IDEOLOGICAL CONTENT IN MY WORK.

"The kitchen, which occupies roughly one-third of the twenty-five-by-ninety-foot space, is the showpiece. It is large and informal, with plenty of work space. The kitchen table, which Buchsbaum designed, exemplifies his resourceful use of materials. Although the top looks like butcher block, it is actually maple floor planks nailed into plywood and cut into free-form curves at one end. The curved end, used as a snack bar, is supported by chrome restaurant table bases bolted to the floor and is surrounded by diner stools. The opposite end is supported by inexpensive metal kitchen cabinets, which provide storage space.

"In addition, there is also a formal dining area. Instead of using conventional tables and chairs, the architect created a raised, carpeted platform with a hole cut in its center, out of which rises a round marble tabletop. Guests sit on the platform with their feet in the hole.

"To make his loft look less long and narrow, Buchsbaum defined the living area by placing a sisal rug on the diagonal. A couple of wood-and-canvas chairs and a cot provide the seating.

"Just behind the dining area are a bedroom and bathroom, raised two feet to hide plumbing and utility lines. The floors of these two rooms are covered with industrial-grade ceramic tiles, chosen for their easy upkeep. Buchsbaum also used the tiles to cover the plywood bed platform.

"Dividing the bedroom and bathroom from a service corridor is a wall made entirely of glass building blocks shaped into a serpentine curve. Because the blocks are translucent, they let in light from the corridor and also give the bedroom area privacy. Another curved glass wall blocks the bathroom from view. The bathroom itself is quite luxurious—there is a marble counter with a mirrored wall above it, and three different kinds of tile in the shower stall. The light fixtures over the counter, as in most of the rest of the loft, are factory lamps."

BUCHSBAUM LOFT 1
THIRD FLOOR

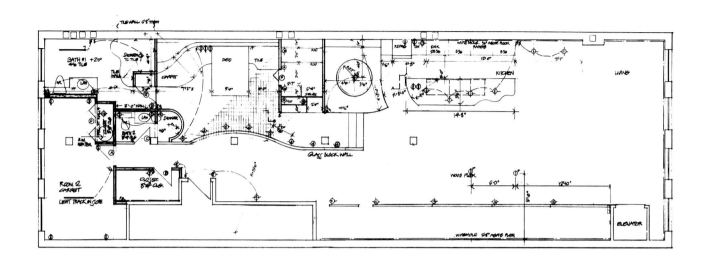

BUCHSBAUM LOFT 2
MEZZANINE, FIRST FLOOR

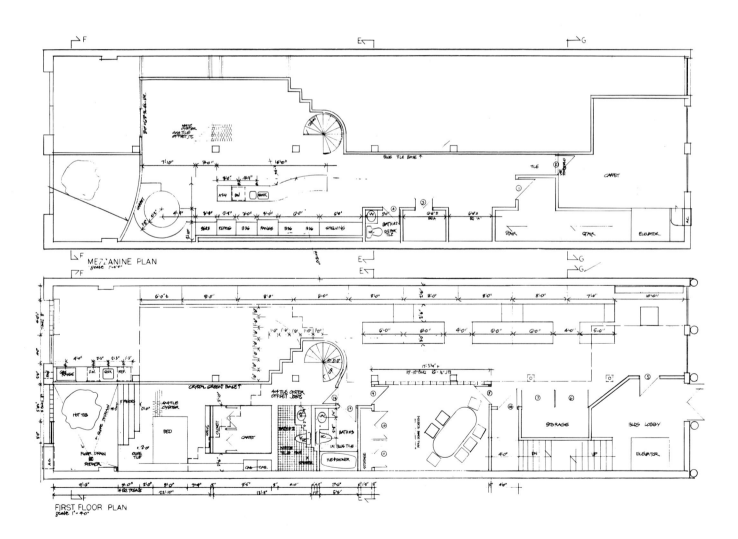

MEZZANINE PLAN

FIRST FLOOR PLAN

BUCHSBAUM LOFT 2

New York, New York
1982

design	Design Coalition: Alan Buchsbaum assisted by Stephen Tilly
photography	Thomas Hooper and Norman McGrath
text	Frederic Schwartz

In 1982 Buchsbaum moved his office and living space to the ground floor loft of 12 Greene Street. He doubled the floor area by inserting a mezzanine level, supported by steel and wood, into the seventeen-foot-high space. The plan and section constantly change from front to back to mask the dual functions of working and living.

The design of the loft reflected both a steady adherence to Modernism and a gravitation toward a romantic use of colors and furnishings. Walls painted in soft pastels were combined with dusty brown velvet upholstery, canvas slipcovers, rich grainy marbles, shiny, industrial black surfaces, and luscious plants. Elegant furnishings from the thirties, original artwork, and new classics were combined with mass-produced, low- and high-tech products. A new ceramic tile floor unified the diverse elements and contrasted with the existing stamped-tin ceiling and raw, heavy timber structure.

EVERY TABLE I DESIGN IS COMPLETELY DIFFERENT. THERE ARE SO MANY MARBLES AVAILABLE THAT IT'S LIKE A PAINTER SAYING HE'S NOT GOING TO USE OIL PAINT OR ACRYLIC PAINT. TO BE CREATIVE TO ME MEANS TO BE DOING SOMETHING THAT YOU HAVEN'T SEEN BEFORE——SO I CHANGE.

The central location of the kitchen, immediately visible upon entry to the mezzanine level, created a theatrical backdrop for food preparation. A chorus line of utensils, equipment, and pots and pans was exposed in the way the rough timber was stripped to reveal the structure of the building. Across from the kitchen counter, the living area was softened by a stepped wall in varying pastel shades that melded into a green curve surrounding a spiral stair. Beyond the kitchen, a built-in "dining sofa" encircled a dramatically illuminated marble slab table.

Also unique was the balcony-like feeling of the mezzanine, which overlooked a luxurious tropical garden complete with a sunken hot tub in the shape of a splash. Downstairs, an open plan (no doors anywhere!) combining bathroom, bedroom, and hot tub was bathed in varying hues of turquoise. Buchsbaum's clever exploitation of single elements with dual functions was in evidence. The wall of the dining banquette became the guardrail for the balcony, the hot tub platform was extended to become a bedside table, and a plumbing-pipe assembly attached to a freestanding wall doubled as a mirrored closet and a divider between bed and bath.

I DON'T WANT TO BE CATEGORIZED; IT'S MORE FUN TO BE ABLE TO PLAY IN ALL THE POOLS.

MILLER KITCHEN

New York, New York
1978

design	Design Coalition: Alan Buchsbaum
photography	Charles Nesbit
text	Frederic Schwartz

Buchsbaum contrasted an enormous nine-by-twelve-foot photo of a dewy Sterling Silver rose with a stark all-white kitchen of plastic laminate cabinets and tile. Buchsbaum called the photo-mural "A Rose Spiral Micro Macro Switch," and added, IT'S ALWAYS A THRILLING EXPERIENCE TO SEE SOMETHING YOU'RE ACCUSTOMED TO SMALL, BLOWN UP TO GIANT SCALE. His signature use of off-the-shelf industrial light fixtures with wavy red cords offers a delicate, whimsical foreground.

ABRAMSON INTERIORS

Camotop, Maryland
1979

design   Design Coalition: Alan Buchsbaum assisted by
                          Gill Anderson and Charles Thanhauser
photography   Norman McGrath
text   Mark Simon

In the late seventies, Charles Moore and I were design-ing a house outside of Washington, D.C. Having designed a "lobsteresque" swinging couch for our client's cousin (never built), our suggestion that we also serve as interior designers for the house was rejected. A search for a sympathetic designer ensued, and through Suzanne Slesin and Dona Guimares of the *New York Times*, I found Alan, whose name I vaguely recognized from Suzanne and Joan Kron's book *High-Tech*. I went to see him in his new Soho loft and there met a kindred spirit. His work was cooler than ours and far more meticulous—more modern and futuristic. But like us, he loved to mix the exquisite with the mundane, the ready-made with the handmade, the cheap with the expensive, and the amusing with the serious.

Alan was rare in that he was confident enough to risk the serendipity of collaboration and enjoy the ride. Together with Charles, the three of us invented many things for the house. Our wallpaper rendered a William Morris pattern in oversized Roy Lichtenstein dots (we called it "Dot's Trellis"—to be spoken with a Lower East Side accent). Just a grid in the dining room, it showed vines in the living room and birds by the time it reached the second floor. A living-room television "tower" cabinet was shaped like an oversized Adam-esque grandfather clock. The mod-ern glass-topped coffee table had a miniature of Michelangelo's Laurentian stairs as its base; other elements were lattice and neon for the dining room chandelier, marble tables with broken edges, solid stone counters that were translucent, and mirrors sandblasted to let light through. His shapes and col-ors, no matter how unusual, were always true. He brought out the best of materials—celebrated them, made you notice them.

Alan became a great friend and my mentor in the art of schmooze. We'd share resources, complain about inept contractors and unruly clients, and most importantly, trade gossip. In that too he was a wonder; he always seemed to know that a journalist would be hired or fired before the journalist did. His gossip was amusing, but it was an education. I'm continually astonished by how much of his work presaged current style (only his was better). Had he lived, he would have taken us further along the way.

run up to plate (roll down hill)

roll around rim of plate →

tunnels through swiss cheese

rocking orange slices

Sand cup

rocking fork

squishy cherries inflated

giant peg

"PLAY SETTING" for NEW ROCHELLE

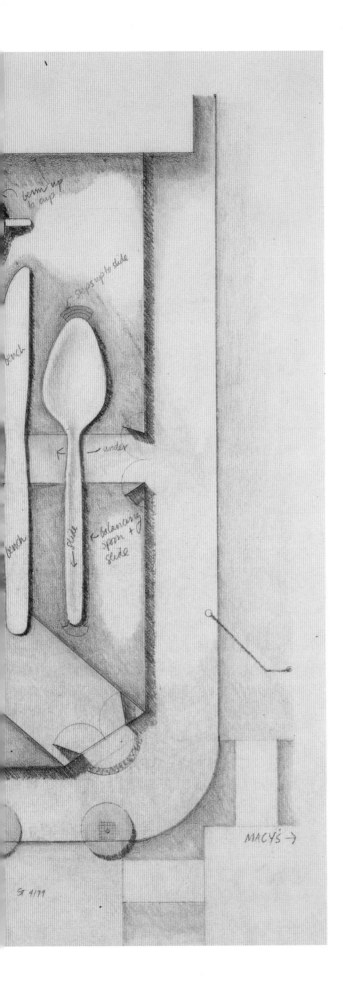

THE PLAY SETTING

New Rochelle, New York
1978

design   Design Coalition: Stephen Tilly with Alan Buchsbaum
and Shelia Berkley
text   Frederic Schwartz

This park was designed for an open ideas competition sponsored by the local Board of Education and Parks Department. The whimsical design includes Oldenberg-like elements: rocking fork, sand cup, bench knife, slide spoon, Swiss cheese tunnels, rocking oranges, inflated cherries, ride-around-the-rim plate edge, and place mat defined by bermed edges. The design was shown in an exhibition, "Urban Open Space," at the Cooper-Hewitt Museum in 1979.

TENENBAUM HOUSE

Columbia, South Carolina
1978

design   Design Coalition: Stephen Tilly and Alan Buchsbaum
photography   Oberto Gili and Norman McGrath
text   Design Coalition

THE TENENBAUM HOUSE IS A 2,500-SQUARE-FOOT PASSIVE-SOLAR RESIDENCE BUILT OF STEEL, GLASS, WOOD, AND CONCRETE ON THE RIGHT BANK OF THE SALUDA RIVER NEAR COLUMBIA, SOUTH CAROLINA. DUE TO ITS PROXIMITY TO THE RIVER, THE HOUSE WAS RAISED ONE STORY ABOVE THE GROUND. IT HAS THE STANDARD COMPLEMENT OF LIVING ROOM, DINING ROOM, KITCHEN, BEDROOMS, AND BATHS. THE SECOND FLOOR IS AN OPEN PLAN MUCH LIKE THE OPEN-PLAN LOFTS OF NEW YORK CITY. THE HOUSE HAS A TROMBE WALL FACING SOUTH MADE OF FILLED CONCRETE BLOCK, PAINTED RED. THE USUAL FOUR-INCH SPACE BETWEEN THE GLASS AND CONCRETE OF A PURE TROMBE WALL WAS WIDENED HERE TO FOUR FEET, AND THE ENTRY STAIRCASE WAS ROUTED THROUGH THE SPACE, MAKING IT A WALK-IN, EASILY MAINTAINED SOLAR COLLECTOR. THE WALL ALSO SERVES AS A LATERAL BRACE FOR THE STEEL STRUCTURE.

SECOND FLOOR

FIRST FLOOR

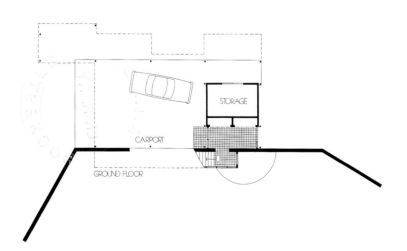

GROUND FLOOR

Samuel tenenbaum is a total extrovert. There is nothing in the least bit recessive about his personality. It never occurred to either him or us to build a quiet little house. We saw no point in trying to be chameleon-like; what better place to be a peacock than in the woods?

STEEL WAS SELECTED TO FRAME THE HOUSE FOR ITS AESTHETIC
QUALITIES AS WELL AS FOR ITS CLEAR SPAN CAPABILITIES. IN
BOTH THE INTERIOR AND THE EXTERIOR, THE STEEL WAS LEFT
EXPOSED AND WAS COLOR-CODED IN HUES OF GREEN ACCORD-
ING TO USE AND TO CONTRAST WITH THE RED TROMBE WALL. IN
ADDITION TO BEING USED FOR THE PRIMARY STRUCTURE, STEEL
ALSO FORMS THE STAIRS AND CATWALK. THE MATERIALS OF THE
LIVING ROOM FURNITURE ARE COLORED WITH VARIOUS SHADES
OF GREEN TO COUNTERPOINT THE RED TROMBE WALL. THE RUG
WAS MADE FROM A PHOTOGRAPH OF A TREE IN THE GARDEN OF
VILLA D'ESTE.

SANJURJO PENTHOUSE

New York, New York
1978

design   Design Coalition: Alan Buchsbaum
photography   Norman McGrath
text   Frederic Schwartz

Eight small rooms on the top floor of a Greenwich Village apartment building became one generous living space with a separate bedroom and bathroom for a theatrical producer. As requested by the client, Buchsbaum focused on daylight, rooftop views, and ideas of sky, air, and brightness.

White paint washed all of the apartment's walls, while a gray grid of preexisting columns, pilasters, and ceiling stripes subdefined "rooms." Bright warm colors applied to the inside of skylights gave character to the entering light and emphasized the ceiling.

Furniture was kept simple and inexpensive as most of the project's budget was directed toward structural change. A prefabricated fireplace—the apartment's focal point—normally installed behind a wall, became a sculptural object between living and dining areas when Buchsbaum and the client agreed that out of the box, its unfinished form, trademark and all, was quite charming.

CANAL STREET SURREALISM
The Sensibility of Alan Buchsbaum

Rosalind Krauss

In 1979 Alan Buchsbaum was asked by a journalist to give his design philosophy. Protesting that he had no such thing, he said only: I AM FASCINATED BY THE MECHANICS OF TASTE.

This fascination ran through a channel that was walled on one side by the legacy of Modernism: its desire for geometry, functionalism, and above all, purity; its horror of ornament, eccentricity, vulgarity. But on the other side was the complex mosaic of stylistic change, particularly as evidenced in the art world, where the sixties were characterized by a succession of alternating styles—wildly opposed sensibilities jostling against one another for attention: Minimalism's aggressive sparseness, Pop Art's clamorous huckster-ism, Fluxus's anarchic clutter, Op Art's marriage of science and psychedelics, Process Art's material form-lessness, Earthwork's laconic gigantism, and Conceptual Art's fastidious irrationality.

The torque set up by this channel exerted a constant pressure on the Modernist idea of taste as universal, on the idea of a rational standard of form that designers should attempt to discover—through pure geometries, through serial logic, through *objets types*—and, once discovered, to enforce. For taste appeared at one and the same time extraordinarily quixotic, and yet for all that, something that could be appealed to in a way that seemed instantly to compel (and sustain) belief. It was this belief, coming as it did from a resource that was more than just fashion, that produced the contradictory "mechanics" so fascinating to Buchsbaum.

There is a detail in the Restivo Apartment (right and pages 116–17) that exemplifies this twist in the grain of taste. It was a very small project, the remodeling of a little one-bedroom apartment; yet he lavished attention on its "idea"—the conception of its space and the relationship of every detail to that conception—in the same way he would pursue the design minutiae of much larger projects. This detail is a floating partition made up of two abutting panes of one-way mirror hung unceremoniously by cables threaded into the glass and suspended from hooks in the ceiling. The blunt directness of the installation and the use of industrial materials—one-way mirror is typically employed on the facades of office buildings, rarely for domestic interiors—coupled with the "less is more"

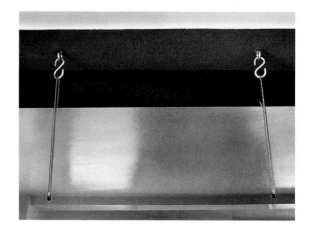

elegance of the six-by-eight-foot rectangle, show Buchsbaum both proficient and canny about the lessons of Modernism. Yet since it is this kind of mirror's nature to sow confusion, those lessons are overturned even while they are paid obeisance.

The one-way mirror performs like a theatrical scrim, a gauze curtain painted with scenery that hangs at the face of the proscenium, providing the actors performing in front of it with a convincing, "opaque" backdrop. But the minute the lights on the main stage go on, the scrim disappears, becoming perfectly transparent to the action behind it. Using tinted glass, however, Buchsbaum's mirror has more the effect of solarized sunglasses, reflective on the luminous side and smokily transparent on the shady one.

The transparent gray rectangle hangs between a small dining area and the living room. On entering the space from the apartment's dark entry hall, the mirror operates not only as a baffle between the observer and the blaze of sunlight pouring through the outsize windows beyond, but also as a picture plane that both frames the distant living space and —there being some light also in the dining area—dimly reflects the contents of the near room, producing the kind of double exposure dear to surrealist photographers, producing the experience of reality-as-image dear to them as well. And from the living room side of the glass, the floating partition functions aggressively as mirror, doubling the space of the room and reflecting the New York skyline, complete with passing clouds, at the same time permitting a vision of only the most luminous objects in the dining area behind it to register on its surface like a strange collection of ghosts.

IT COMPLICATES THE IMAGES, Buchsbaum said of the mirror. And to complicate them further he designed a richly veined, highly polished, marble dining table in the shape of a pear, to create simultaneously a trick perspective—the far side steeply narrowing relative to the near one—and another "mirror" surface. The clouds reflecting onto the pear, and both of them then reflecting into the partition, produce an effect he found extremely satisfying: LIKE MAGRITTE.

The references to Magritte and to Surrealism take us across the divide that was set up in the 1920s between Modernism's rational, functionalist architecture and its irrationalist opponents. Referring to Le Corbusier's mechanistic ideal as "that aesthetics of castration," Tristan Tzara attacked Modernism. Both he and André Breton saw it as suppressing the life of the interior psyche, producing "a solidification of desire in a most violent and cruel automatism."[1] Instead they supported the ideas of an artist like Louis Soutter who said, "The minimum house or future cell should be in translucent glass. No more windows, these useless eyes. Why look outside?" Le Corbusier was shocked by such a notion: "This affirmation of Louis Soutter . . . is the very antithesis of my own ideas, but it manifests the intense interior life of the thinker."[2]

The Belgian surrealist René Magritte had repeatedly made pictures of the "interior life of the thinker," as in his 1927 painting *The False Mirror*—a close-up of a staring eye, its pupil a black circle, the white of the eye an immense cloudscape. This was not unrelated to the rationalist architectural tradition, inevitably recalling Claude-Nicolas Ledoux's famous Enlightenment image of an eye facing forward, its iris and pupil strangely transparent to the scene of an amphitheater projected within the orbit of the eyeball, simultaneously the perspective onto which the eye might be looking and the image of the architect's mental conception of the vista. But Magritte's limitless sky did not gesture toward the rationality and logic of what goes on behind the eye's facade. It addressed the irrational leaps of thought and of dream.

In 1958 Magritte made a different image of "thinking," a picture of an open umbrella with a water glass perched on top of it. In a letter to a friend he described the process through which these two objects came to be juxtaposed, ending with: "I think Hegel would have liked this object that has two contradictory functions: to repel and contain water. Wouldn't that have amused him as we are amused when on vacation?"[3] Accordingly he called the picture *Hegel's Vacation.*

This matter of windowless rooms and the "interior life of the thinker" came together in Buchsbaum's work in a 1984 model-room project for Casa Tile (right and pages 146–47), a room to which he gave the name "Hegel's Vacation." One problem typical of any designer's model room is that it is hopelessly cut off from any possibility of a window onto the outside world, and so although designers usually present a domestic interior—kitchen, study, bath, playroom—their problem is to mask the fact of its location at the very center of the showroom floor. "Hegel's Vacation," however, happily declared its place in the bowels of the labyrinth, pronouncing itself as much stage set as room by leaving off the ceiling of the philosopher's study, thus making the ducts and lighting track of the commercial space completely visible above the pristine walls of the "room." Further, instead of masking the room's openings onto a wholly fictitious outside, either by presenting the corner of a space that has no windows (a breakfast nook, for example) or by discreetly lowering blinds or closing shutters, "Hegel's Vacation" is *about* the punctures in its back wall, for its main design event is the set of broken-terra-cotta-tile frames that surround its window and door. And the view out the window is not finessed but defiantly presented: a black-and-white photograph of a turbulent cloudscape. The only other things in the room are also black and white: the strange multi-legged table in black-and-white wood-grained Formica, the desk chair that looks as if a black-and-white patterned sheet had been thrown over it, and the black umbrella lying on the floor in front of the table—on which, not surprisingly, there sat a glass of water.

Two years earlier Buchsbaum had opened his relation to Casa Tile (a consortium of Italian tile manufacturers) with this same refusal to simulate a functional room, and the same desire to float the "room" within the unreality of an unlocatable interior/exterior. To this end he constructed a tile patio surrounded by a low parapet (right and pages 144–45). At the near end a red-and-black Isuzu motorcycle was parked; at the far end two blue wicker chairs companionably faced out onto the expanse beyond: the photomural of an open sky with a few hawks wheeling through it making patterns of dark Vs against the clouds. Nothing could have been less clear than what and where this space was supposed to be. For the illusion was that the patio must be a kind of aerie, perched high atop a granite cliff. The effect was startlingly thrilling, especially since the only "design" Buchsbaum had allowed himself was the regular geometric pattern of the patio's tiles, pushed into irregularity by the subtle color shifts and the kind of palette that had by then become his stock in trade: here a combination of mustards, mauves, ochers, and greens, an ensemble that sounds plausible enough but in the actual fact pushed ever so resolutely toward the outer limits of "good" taste. As he explained: I'M NOT CRAZY ABOUT THE CLICHÉD NEW YORK–STYLE APARTMENT— BEIGE, SHINY, AND WELL-COORDINATED. WHEN I DESIGN A ROOM, I WANT PEOPLE TO LOOK AT IT AND ASK, "WHAT'S WRONG WITH THIS PICTURE?"[4]

It is the jarring note, whether through a color that is "off," or a peculiarly draped fabric, or a skewed perspective, that produces, however, a sense that one is not so much seeing the space before one's eyes as remembering it. And it is that effect of memory that Buchsbaum opened himself to. It is there in the resolutely anti-Modernist Modernist furniture that Buchsbaum designed, beginning with the slipcovers he made to look like sheets thrown over sofas and chairs (above) as when, in the Savannah home of his childhood, the house was closed up for the summer when the family moved to the beach. He once said: THE DAY THAT WE CAME BACK TO TOWN WAS A BIG DAY FOR ME. I LOVED WALKING INTO THE HOUSE AND SEEING ALL THE FURNITURE COVERED WITH SHEETS. He explained to his interlocutor that the front of a slipcover must of course be carefully measured to the floor and fitted to the seat. He continued: BUT ON THE BACK, WHERE NOTHING HAPPENS, ANYTHING CAN HAPPEN. THE COVER CAN HAVE ALL THE FLAIR AND FANTASY OF DRACULA'S CAPE. Clearly, this was the idea of a slipcover gone on Hegel's vacation.

Buchsbaum produced other furniture off on the same type of holiday, the strange marriage of unlikely partners that the Surrealists had admired in another image celebrating an umbrella: Lautréamont's poetic figure of the fortuitous encounter of a sewing machine and an umbrella on a dissecting table. "Exquisite corpse" was another name for the Surrealists' fondness for the concatenation of heterogeneous bits and pieces to add up to a mysterious and irrational whole. And Buchsbaum excelled in the furniture of the "exquisite corpse," such as the various bases he found for his beloved wicker chairs: a set of Queen Anne legs, a cantilevered spring base of tubular steel.

One of the great sources the Surrealists had recourse to for their own production of "fortuitous encounters" was the Paris flea market. There the undertow of capitalism had exerted itself on the field of commodity, the current cycle of fashion rendering a given wave of goods outmoded and, sucking it under, washing over it a newer, shinier version. The reef onto which these obsolete goods would subsequently surface as so much flotsam and jetsam, the discards of so many different fields of spent desire, was the flea market. It was there that the Surrealists imagined objects calling out to them for possession for purposes as yet undreamed of by the potential owner. It was there that they "recoded" these objects by bestowing on them an entirely different use and meaning from the one for which they had originally been manufactured. Thus refusing to accept the world of consumer goods as presented to them by the powers of industry and manufacture, the Surrealists were the first, in Walter Benjamin's eyes, "to perceive the revolutionary energies that appear in the 'outmoded.'"[5]

And indeed, across from the loft building in Soho where Buchsbaum moved his practice in the mid-seventies, there was an active, cacophonous flea market, adding its load of old furniture and crockery to the already eccentric possibilities of the great used-hardware stores that still lined Canal Street at that time. In the late sixties Sol LeWitt used to speak of Eva Hesse's "shopping sprees" on Canal Street, where she would buy mountains of rubber washers, lengths of plastic tubing, and long sheets of latex, bringing it all back to her studio in triumph to begin experimenting.

Buchsbaum had begun the decade of the seventies with a shinier sense of hardware than Hesse's. Working with industrial shelving and lighting elements, with pipe lengths and ready-made commercial elements like chrome lunch-counter pedestals, he had pioneered the design sensibility that would come to be called "High-Tech." But no sooner did a book of that name appear than Buchsbaum jumped this particular fashion ship, to move toward the funkier, more perversely imaginative version of Canal Street sensibility that Hesse had inhabited.

It became very clear to him that he had to sound the depths of his own unconscious, his memories, his fantasies, to produce forms that would go far beyond the ready-made's appeal to memory—our sense of all the other contexts, many of them in the past, in which we've experienced those commercial or industrial parts—and would instead organize an image: sometimes disturbing, sometimes elusive, sometimes deeply comforting.

The example that comes to mind is a hearth rug (right and page 159) that Buchsbaum designed to be placed in front of an ornate fireplace. Long and thin, like an Oriental runner, the rug, in the intense green of freshly mown grass, is contoured in very low relief to produce the image of a "pillow" set a bit askew at one end and a slight incursion of the suggestion of a wave at the "foot" end of the rug—an undulation of black bordering an eccentric band of brilliant blue. The image that is produced by this object is at one and the same time the suggestion of the body stretched out in front of the fire, having imported a pillow from the couches above to make itself comfortable on the rug below, and—defying the context in which we find this object—the body lying on a beach towel, head nestled into the softness of the sand, feet pointed resolutely toward the surf. The rug's image thus incongruously marries heat with wetness, inside with outside, darkness with sunlight. But bridging these opposites is the underlying metaphor of the object, which is that bodies leave their traces on the objects they use, particularly those they love, those that served as the sites of their pleasures.

Curiously, this "pillow rug" encapsulates in a single object the feel of a stage setting designed over fifty years earlier by Le Corbusier: the penthouse terrace of the De Beistegui apartment (1930–1931). There, two nineteenth-century iron garden chairs face each other in front of a marble fireplace set into the face of the wall that bounds the terrace's lawn. In a famous photograph of this grouping, pillows are arranged in front of and to one side of the fireplace, and over the top of the wall one can glimpse the top of the Arch de Triomphe, just enough of it visible to see that its shape rhymes with the arch of the marble chimney piece.

Writing about a design such as this, in which Le Corbusier abandons the hard rationalism and exclusionary purity of his city plans, the architectural historian Colin Rowe sees a concession to what he calls a collage sensibility. "It is a commentary upon exclusiveness," he says. "For collage, often a method of paying attention to the left-overs of the world, of preserving their integrity and equipping them with dignity, of compounding matter of fact and cerebrallity, as a convention and a breach of convention, necessarily operates unexpectedly."[6]

The very title of Rowe's important book *Collage City* (1978) acknowledges an alternative to hard-core architectural Modernism, seeing an important aesthetic resource in the neighboring visual arts, a resource that allows architects to acknowledge the actual, heterogeneous textures of cities, a result of their openness to mutation and change: "The tradition of modern architecture, always professing a distaste for art, has characteristically conceived of society and the city in highly conventional artistic terms—unity, continuity, system; but the alternative and apparently far more 'art'-prone method of procedure has, so far as one can see, never felt any need for such literal alignment with 'basic' principles. The alternative and predominant tradition of modernity has always made a virtue of irony, obliquity, and multiple reference."[7]

Something of a manifesto on behalf of a collage-based sensibility, the text surveys the experiential results of collage's operations as they are carried out by Picasso's famous *Still Life with Chair Caning* (1912) or his *Bull's Head* (1944), made from a bicycle seat joined to a set of handlebars: "Remembrance of former function and value (bicycles and minotaurs); shifting context; an attitude which encourages the composite; an exploitation and re-cycling of meaning (has there ever been enough to go around?); desuetude of function with corresponding agglomeration of reference; memory; anticipation; the connectedness of memory and wit; the integrity of wit." And Rowe then goes on to speak of the lesson architects might draw from this collage proposition: "Since it is a proposition evidently addressed to people, it is in terms such as these, in terms of pleasures remembered and desired, of a dialectic between past and future, of an impacting of iconographic content, of a temporal as well as a spatial collision, that . . . one might proceed to specify an ideal city of the mind."[8]

There is an important distinction to be made between *Collage City* and the earlier manifesto by Robert Venturi, *Complexity and Contradiction in Architecture* (1966). Venturi's attack on Modernism, purity, rationality—his countering of Mies's famous "less is more" with his own "less is a bore"—was in the name of values that were ultimately associated with Pop Art. And this Pop sensibility with its raiding of trademark styles gradually evolved into the historicist eclecticism, the recycling of anti-Modern idioms, that became architectural Post-modernism. The position taken by *Collage City* is not that of an ironic, Pop relation to styles, but rather the belief in collage as its own powerful style, no matter how hybrid its components.

And it is just this collage approach that Alan Buchsbaum found himself adopting as he delved deeper and deeper into his own design convictions. Martin Filler described his path during the eighties as independent of current design battles: "His late designs embody implicit critiques of the rigid, diagrammatic quality common to much Late Modern and Postmodern design alike. His refusal to supplant one dogmatic approach with another placed him outside critical attention to an extent that now seems surprising in light of the consistently high standard of his output. But there was at least one benefit to Buchsbaum's distance from the ideological fray: he was able to develop his ideas without undue concern for extraneous matters."9

The course he steered was into the heart of his own sensibility, an eccentric but sure sense of the very mechanics of "taste" that had always fascinated him. It is extremely hard to pinpoint that taste. One could call it Canal Street Surrealism. But I prefer to return to Colin Rowe's characterization of the rewards of collage: "of pleasures remembered and desired, of a dialectic between past and future, of an impacting of iconographic content, of a temporal as well as a spatial collision." All of this perfectly mobilized is what marked Alan Buchsbaum's work.

1. Anthony Vidler, *The Architectural Uncanny* (Cambridge, Mass.: MIT Press, 1992), 151.

2. Le Corbusier, "Louis Soutter: L'inconnue de la soixantaine," *Minotaure* 9 (October 1936): 62.

3. Cited by Harry Torczyner, *Magritte: Ideas and Images* (New York: Harry N. Abrams, 1977), 259.

4. Quoted in *Metropolitan Home,* September 1982, 62.

5. Walter Benjamin, *Reflections,* trans. Edmund Jephcott (New York: Harcourt Brace Jovanovich, 1978), 181.

6. Colin Rowe and Fred Koetter, *Collage City* (Cambridge, Mass.: MIT Press, 1978), 142.

7. Rowe and Koetter, *Collage City,* 138.

8. Rowe and Koetter, *Collage City,* 138.

9. Martin Filler, "Eye of His Times," *Architectural Record Interiors,* 1987, 110.

RESTIVO APARTMENT

New York, New York
1979

design	Design Coalition: Alan Buchsbaum
photography	Oberto Gili
text	Frederic Schwartz

The design of this small, one-bedroom apartment in midtown Manhattan illustrates Buchsbaum's conceptual thinking and multidisciplinary approach, which combined theater, lighting, and the juxtaposition of materials and objects. IT IS DEFINITELY THEATRICAL. WE WANTED TO GO FROM TOTAL DARKNESS INTO A MEDIUM LIGHT, AND THEN TO A VERY BRIGHT ZONE; TO DELINEATE THE SPACES AS A PROGRESSION OF SEQUENTIAL LIGHT DENSITIES.

The drama and surrealistic quality of this project are generated by a ceiling-hung one-way mirror (TO COMPLICATE THE IMAGES) that separates the gray-zone dining room from the large-windowed, white-zone living room. Objects placed near the mirror mysteriously become reflected still lifes. Lighting controlled by dimmers is used to modify the reflectivity in the evening as the light and mood change. The bright, white living room and its counterpoints (an antique chair reupholstered in yellow-orange canvas and modern lamps with exposed cords) are seen both as reflections and through the glass. The soft curves of Buchsbaum's signature pear-shaped table contrast with its hard, polished marble surface. WE THOUGHT THE APARTMENT WAS GETTING TOO SERIOUS. I FELT THAT THE FRUIT SHAPE WAS A LITTLE SILLY BUT THAT IF IT WAS CONTRASTED WITH THE TEXTURE AND GRAINY MATERIAL OF THE GREEN MARBLE, IT COULD SUCCEED. In contrast to the public zones, the bedroom is a simple, serene, Zen-like space bathed in an aura of very cool blue light.

SUCH A LOT OF GOOD DESIGN COMES ABOUT BY ACCIDENT ANYWAY. THE PASSAGE FROM TWO-DIMENSIONAL REALITY IS FRAUGHT WITH MANY DELIGHTFUL DETOURS AND SURPRISING RESOLUTIONS.

HIRSCH KITCHEN

New York, New York
1979

design	Design Coalition: Alan Buchsbaum
	assisted by German Martinez
photography	Charles Nesbit
text	Marilyn Bethany, "High-Tech Style Goes Glamorous"

By 1980 some significant changes were taking place in high-tech design. To the very industrial decors of the seventies a touch of luxury was being applied; Buchsbaum was leading the field with projects, such as the Hirsch Kitchen, that were regularly published in leading periodicals. Writer Marilyn Bethany documented this Upper East Side project for the *New York Times Magazine:*

"The familiar elements of the 'high-tech' style are present in force—glass-block windows, restaurant stove, industrial lamps, coffee-shop shelving, plenty of stainless steel. Yet the kitchen is not high-tech as we have known it in the past. Gone is the no-nonsense functionalism. Absent, too, are many of the economies that made high-tech so accessible. What remains is the fundamental soundness of the design, but glamorized.

"The look is dazzling. Unexpected materials warm the steel and tile iciness. The tiles are not the slick ceramic kind usually associated with high-tech; instead, they are the rough, warm, Mexican type. Glittering mirror backsplashes lift coffee-shop shelving to heretofore unattained heights of elegance. Bentwood chairs and a long wood table, as well as a wood-framed mirror retrieved from an old luncheonette, give the dining area a note of well-worn warmth.

"Bright touches of brass abound: sandblasted industrial lampshades have been dipped in the yellow metal, a band of which borders the restaurant-stove hood. Even the conventional handles on the wall ovens have been replaced with brass towel bars. As a result of this buildup of brass, such normally unnotable elements as the locks on the fire door (the standard, prewar, steel variety with paint removed) become important points in the decor."

GERBER/ROTHBERG APARTMENT

New York, New York
1979

design   Alan Buchsbaum
photography   Oberto Gili
text   Frederic Schwartz

The clients had strong ideas about the image they wanted to project, as well as a highly cultivated appreciation for furnishings, objects, and industrial components, which Buchsbaum used, like a set designer, to style a Parisian-like atmosphere. The overall effect was a sophisticated mix of everyday objects set in deliberate juxtapositions.

The architectural backdrop was bright, elegant, and neutral; natural light encouraged views into adjacent spaces. All doors were steel and glass except those in the bathroom and bedrooms; all walls and ceilings were painted white. The apartment's rich diversity of furnishings was counterposed against a subtle and disciplined use of glass block, tile patterns, and orthogonal placement of furniture.

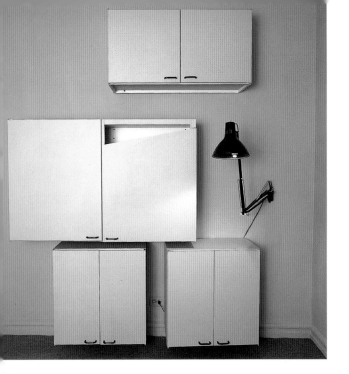

JAKOBSON BEDROOM

New York, New York
1980

design   Alan Buchsbaum
photography   Charles Nesbit
text   Barbara Jakobson

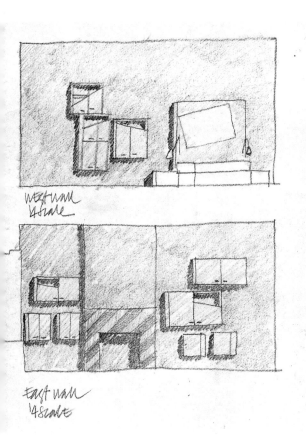

west wall
¼ scale

east wall
¼ scale

Buchsbaum described this room as punk and strange due to his random placement of cabinets, which protrude from the walls and appear to fly around the room with no rhyme or reason. Buchsbaum designed a number of small projects, and of this Upper East Side bedroom for a close friend, Barbara Jakobson, the owner writes:

"Alan's room was repainted last week—the same vibrant blue. It remains exactly as it was when it was designed for my then-teenage daughter in 1980. The program was 'do something to get all her stuff off the floor for virtually no money.' Without breaking a wall, a traditional brownstone bedroom, with its Victorian marble fireplace, plaster moldings, and exposed-pipe bathroom, was totally transformed by placing the bed and stock Formica kitchen cabinets at angles to the walls, intersecting the room with a red-painted beam that holds a light fixture, and designing a mattress platform with two low tables covered in onyx.

"As I stood in the room this morning, I remembered Alan explaining how its rather boring narrowness would come alive by skewing the space—this achieved by putting wood wedges of varying widths behind the cabinets and adding a red diagonal on the ceiling. So, I thought, I had a deconstructivist room before the term had even come into the architectural lexicon! That was Alan."

THE LOOK OF THE EIGHTIES IS POLYCHROME. NOT HOMOGENEOUS DESIGN, BUT A MIXTURE OF DESIGNS; INFLUENCES FROM MALEVICH AND KANDINSKY. WHAT I HOPE HAPPENS IS THAT HISTORICAL REFERENCE IN ARCHITECTURE AND DESIGN WILL COMBINE WITH MODERNISM OR WILL FADE OUT. I WAS BROUGHT UP UNDER THE PRINCIPLES OF THE BAUHAUS AND THEY ARE MY RELIGION—I AM NOT A HISTORICIST.

THE DIVINE MR. B

from *Metropolis,* 1983

Patricia Leigh Brown

If all the world's a stage and the men merely players, Alan Buchsbaum is the guy waiting in the wings with the hook. He has little tolerance for boredom. In 1973, to supplement his architectural practice, Buchsbaum took to writing restaurant reviews under the pseudonym "FAT" for the *Village Voice.* Not content merely to eat, he proceeded to get himself hired as a waiter at Raoul's. Not content merely to review, he wrote a series of vignettes in which FAT's persona alternated between an Agatha Christie–style mystery writer and an architectural critic ("Captain Marvel couldn't have done with a basement what Gwathmey and Siegel have done with Shezan," the perspicacious FAT noted). EVERY RESTAURANT WAS DIFFERENT, EVERY OWNER WAS DIFFERENT, THE FOOD WAS DIFFERENT, Buchsbaum now explains of his temporary foray into journalism. Buchsbaum was merely being Buchsbaum—stretching himself, being different. Some might say eccentric.

At age forty-seven, Alan Buchsbaum is considered one of the most versatile and idiosyncratic designers in New York. Known for a witty, provocative style that ranges over wide territory—from furniture design to interiors for celebrities like Bette Midler and Diane Keaton—Buchsbaum is an architect who relishes contradictions. Like Shakespeare's mischievous Puck, whom he somewhat resembles physically, Buchsbaum delights in rearranging life's givens, bringing odd couples together—English chintz with Italian sofas, marble tabletops with plumber's pipes, television sets with mock–Robert Adam frames.

At Case Tile '82, the Italian Trade Commission's tile show last spring, Buchsbaum's entry, "6-5-4-3-2-1 Wyoming," was a cockeyed interpretation of a desert landscape, consisting of a photographic wall mural of flying birds, two wicker chairs, a motorcycle, and a rhythmically patterned floor of sand- and brown-colored tile (pages 144–45). I KNEW EVERYBODY ELSE WAS GOING TO GO AFTER FLOWERS, FRUIT, AND CANDY, says Buchsbaum. He does not enjoy "nice" or "sweet" design.

Although Buchsbaum is considered something of a maverick among New York architects, in part because his work is associated more with interior design than with architecture, this in no way lessens his influence. "Alan has made a major statement about relaxing things," observes architect Mark Simon, who along with partner Charles Moore, recently collaborated with Buchsbaum on a house (a house that featured a Buchsbaum-designed coffee table with an unusual base—a replica of the Laurentian Library stairs). "Not only is he a damn good designer, but he takes chances others won't take."

If Buchsbaum's iconoclastic designs make a major statement about relaxing things, part of that comes from his own personal style. He insists, for example, that anyone who seeks to understand his work must talk to people who don't like it—and provides a list complete with phone numbers. Buchsbaum is full of interesting contrasts: a Jewish boy educated at a Catholic military academy; an architect to glamorous clients who's in bed by 10:30 every night; a laconic southerner with a finger so close to the pulse of the culture that it is Alan Buchsbaum editors call to find out what's happening in New York.

Among his other qualities, he's a schmoozer. He's constantly calling people on the phone: "Somehow, Alan has convinced every editor in New York that she's his best friend," in the words of one highly placed design writer. He loves to gossip. I HAVE SOMETHING FUNNY TO TELL YOU, he'll say as he calls people like Joan Kron and Marilyn Bethany to exchange views about the whys and wherefores of design in New York. One of his many well-known admirers, Bethany, of the *New York Times,* says of his casual, funky style, "I sort of think of Alan as a Hawaiian shirt, flapping in the breeze."

His reputation as a gadfly is not attended by pejorative overtones. This is because it reflects a singular talent: an ability to communicate. Such are the challenges of interpreting the built environment in the press that it's no wonder the articulate and accessible Buchsbaum gets quoted. One of the qualities that distinguishes his work and personality is an ability to draw from the world around him on the one hand and draw out the world around him on the other.

Unlike many architects who adhere to rigid formulas or impose prefab solutions on clients, there's a free give-and-take between Alan Buchsbaum and the universe. He take trends seriously, whether he's soaking up the art scene in Soho or the tele-imagery of cable's MTV. It's no accident that his clients consist of live wires with their own ideas—people like his old friend Bette Midler, who calls him "a doll with great imagination and flair." The ability to collaborate creatively may be one of Alan Buchsbaum's greatest gifts. He explained recently: I'M NOT A PURIST. AN ITALIAN MAGAZINE JUST WROTE ASKING ME TO EXPLAIN MY PHILOSO- PHY. I DON'T HAVE A PHILOSOPHY! EVERYTHING I DO IS INTUITIVE. I DESIGN TO PROVOKE COMMENT. I WANT TO MAKE PEOPLE LAUGH, FEEL AT EASE. I JUDGE GOOD ARCHITECTURE BY THE EMOTIONAL EXPERIENCE IT EVOKES.

His allergic reaction to dogmas came early. Born in Savannah, Buchsbaum was weaned on "the Mies van der Rohe experience" at Georgia Tech and MIT. Although he feels at home with the work of Charles Moore, Alvar Aalto, and Frank Gehry, architects of whom he's particularly fond, Buchsbaum has never allied himself to a particular school. His use of bright colors, playful shapes, and historical references elicits the term *Postmodernism* from some critics—YOU CAN ANALYZE THINGS UP TO A POINT AND THEN YOU'RE BETTER OFF NOT FOOLING WITH THEM, he says in response. Also, Buchsbaum has never had a mentor, prompting Marilyn Bethany to remark that he is "one of the few architects around who seems to have gotten over his education."

Certainly nobody could accuse his most recent work of being perfect or pure. Take the office he designed last year for successful television commercial producer Gennaro Andreozzi, for instance (pages 142–43). More an architectural collage than a typical-looking office, it's full of quirky design elements, from the front desk, which combines Formica and Styrofoam with a purpleheart wood molding, to a slate- and quarry-tile checkerboard wall that surrounds an old wooden loft window (right). Nontraditional colors, materials, textures, and shapes converge: a coral-hued onyx conference table (with nine legs) surrounded by Bank of England chairs painted punk red, glass block, velvet curtains, Yankee Stadium bleachers, and illustrated outdoor billboard lights are all used with aplomb. Even traditional materials in traditional contexts—bathroom tiles, for instance—become non sequiturs when placed together in unfamiliar patterns of lavenders, peaches, yellows, greens, beiges, and whites.

The feeling of things being slightly askew is the result of considerable forethought: I THINK OF THE SPACE AS IMPLYING "WHAT'S WRONG WITH THIS PICTURE?" Buchsbaum has said. The high contrast is intentional. Although extremely unconventional, it's a solution appropriate to the client: "We're not a bank, we're contemporary creative people," Andreozzi explains. "I'd spent all my life in pseudo-Bauhaus agencies—they get boring." After a year in Buchsbaum's space, Andreozzi says, "We still walk around and look at it— it has that much interest built into it. The clients love it and it's livable." An employee of Andreozzi's pays Buchsbaum probably the greatest compliment: "This office keeps people from getting on each other's nerves," she says.

Buchsbaum once had a go at the traditional architect's route. Fresh out of school, he worked on designs for the city center of Reston, Virginia, while at Conklin Rossant in 1961. He then took a job with Warner Burn Toan Lunde designing the Princeton Mathematics Building, a project that was rather unsatisfying since he was forced to design the building in their form. Afterwards, he bought an airline ticket and spent a year traveling around the world looking at cities. Returning to New York broke and in debt, he got a job offer from another large architectural firm. Something clicked: I LOOKED OUT OVER THE SEA OF DRAFTING TABLES, AND I KNEW THAT GOING TO WORK AT A FIRM LIKE THAT WOULD BE LIKE SQUEEZING TOOTHPASTE BACK INTO THE TUBE. IT WAS IMPOSSIBLE. Out of sheer frustration, insanity, and willpower, he struck out on his own and founded Design Coalition, a multidisciplinary Soho-based firm, in 1967.

Much of the Coalition's work has included interiors, which tend to be small, personal spaces that allow Buchsbaum to get involved in the totality of the work. He deliberately complicates things to keep his interest up, getting engrossed in details such as the design of furniture and wallpaper, which many architects don't bother with. He likens his role to that of a character actor rather than a star, a foil that modulates or changes into whatever persona is required. As a result, notes Joan Kron, "Alan has never had a reproducible look or signature. He's not a Joe D'Urso with a clearly definable style or a tendency toward sharp edges or refined images. You usually don't walk into a room and say, 'Oh, that's Alan Buchsbaum.'"

Buchsbaum himself would cringe at the label "Alan Buchsbaum." EVERYBODY FEELS SO MUCH BETTER WHEN THEY CAN LUMP YOU INTO A CATEGORY, he says, bemused. One category into which Buchsbaum has been placed in recent years is High-Tech. Buchsbaum's use of Hubbell obstruction lights with blue bulbs simulating airport lights (page 77), glass block, and restaurant stools made him a leading figure in Kron and Suzanne Slesin's design bible, *High-Tech*. (Quips Buchsbaum: HIGH-TECH DIDN'T EXIST UNTIL THAT BOOK CAME OUT.) Although his work has changed considerably from those days, when his serpentine glass walls and tiled floors tended toward an inspired sterility, he continues to be associated with the trend to some extent: I LOST A JOB RECENTLY. A WOMAN CALLED ME UP AND TOLD ME I WAS TOO HIGH-TECH.

Despite his protestation, certain aspects of the High-Tech sensibility —a reaction against preciousness, the pursuit of relaxed, comfortable living spaces, a respect for "found" materials—still ring true. And some favorite Buchsbaum design elements, such as Holophane lamps (page 76), marble tables floating on painted plumber's pipes, and Bank of England chairs (favored for their comfort, solidity, sculptural qualities, and for a time, their low cost), come out of this era (right).

Eclecticism continues to be a hallmark of his work, particularly in furniture design, an area he's currently trying to "un-define." "If there's a box, Alan will change it," observes Miltiodes Mandros, a woodworker with whom Buchsbaum collaborates. "Alan doesn't think rectangles; he thinks triangles and intersecting planes." Buchsbaum's approach is definitely that of an architect: his furniture evolves out of spatial concepts. A polished green marble table in the shape of a pear, for example, was triggered by the Restivo Apartment (page 116–17), which was designed in an abstract conceptual manner, including a one-way mirror and rooms that were color-coded according to light. Buchsbaum explained: I SOMEHOW FELT, AS I ALWAYS DO, THAT THE APARTMENT WAS TOO SERIOUS—THAT WE NEEDED A JOKE IN IT. THE PEAR IS A VERY BEAUTIFUL SHAPE AND, SOMEHOW, IT FIT THE APARTMENT. The pear itself evolved as Buchsbaum and a partner began drawing the table in perspective and discovered that "it sort of got smaller" at the far end. WE LEARNED THE TABLE DIDN'T NEED TO BE A PERFECT GEOMETRIC SHAPE, AND THAT OPENED UP A WHOLE RANGE OF POSSIBILITIES.

Buchsbaum, an aficionado of Magritte and Man Ray, has a graphic sensibility as well as a perverse, out-of-context quality of work that includes a surrealistic play between illusion and reality. (His predilection for pop "super-graphics," such as his now-famous blow-up of Charles Nesbit's rose on the wall of the Miller Kitchen, goes back to the mid-sixties; page 92–93.) He recently designed a whirlpool bath in the shape of a splash (page 91). Such designs have prompted some observers to liken him to a conceptual artist. It's as if Buchsbaum were a Russian doll—open the architect, you'll find a designer; open the designer, you'll find an artist. One doesn't really know what will pop up next.

Client Lynn Grossman, a screen and comedy writer married to actor Bob Balaban, views Buchsbaum as "having essentially the mind and eye of a child; he sees shapes and colors that grown-ups don't see." In Buchsbaum's world Holophane lamps become sculptural objects, suspended to look as though they're capable of hanging from a drooping cord. The furniture Buchsbaum has designed for Grossman and Balaban's Upper West Side apartment is full of the sensual, "child-like" qualities Grossman admires (pages 154–57). Catering to her fear of not having enough places to seat people, Buchsbaum is in the process of creating a four-piece buffet of white and gray Formica, part of which can extend onto the two-piece granite dining-room table. A "gallery table" (right) for paintings will combine three different surfaces: Sardinian white granite, pale yellow Formica, and French rose marble: THE COLOR OF TOMATO SOUP WITH GRAY CLOUDS IN IT, says Buchsbaum. The apartment will also include a built-in banquette and lawn chairs with pink cushions. There won't be a perfect shape in the place, except for, perhaps, the piano. "When I first saw Alan's designs," Grossman now admits, "I thought he was out of his mind."

Buchsbaum's own highly developed sense of humor seems to be brought out by clients like Grossman, whom he admires in turn for her "Rodney Dangerfield" sensibility "that lets her come up with statement A and arrive at solution M." Buchsbaum himself seems to be consistently arriving at solution M. There is definitely an edge to his humor, a jagged quality reminiscent of the rough edges of his furniture. Something is invariably left hanging, unsettled—like an untied shoe, or a door ajar, or . . . a fly in one's soup. Certainly not every client knows what to make of Buchsbaum at his most whimsical. The Laurentian Library coffee table (page 94) and Robert Adam television tower (opposite) designed for a collaborative venture with Mark Simon and Charles Moore (the house was Japanese Tudor, according to Moore) proved to be too much for the client, for example, although the client did decide to keep the Italian sofa clad in English chintz.

Even the most "playful" clients, such as the Divine Miss M, have limits. Buchsbaum's original color scheme was "too bright," Midler says. "In my personal life, I'm really very tasteful, quiet, and serene." Buchsbaum admits his designs may strike people in a way that some offbeat fashions do—something you like to look at but don't necessarily want to own. Not everyone can handle solution M.

Buchsbaum has his own theory about where his penchant for "amusing" design comes from: BASICALLY, I'M MOROSE. SO LAUGHTER IS THE GREATEST TREASURE I CAN FIND. He sees a lot of black humor in his work—I'M NOT POLLYANNA. As a close friend observes, one gets the sense that Buchsbaum's tragicomic wit, like that of many of the world's best clowns and funny people, comes from an innate suspicion that "basically, life is terrible, which makes you more inclined to laugh than if it's terrifying." So it's not surprising that Buchsbaum gravitates to designs that are "life-affirming," Charles Moore's neon-lit Piazza d'Italia in New Orleans, for example, which he calls MORE THRILLING THAN THE FONTANA DI TREVI. Buchsbaum would like to design a piazza someday, even an entire town like Reston. Someday soon. WHEN I WAS YOUNGER, I NEVER UNDERSTOOD THE THEORY THAT AN ARCHITECT HAS TO BE FIFTY BEFORE HE REALLY GETS TO BE ANY GOOD, BUT NOW I UNDERSTAND WHAT IT'S ABOUT. YOU CAN'T REALLY GET THE EXPERIENCE OF HAVING DONE ENOUGH WORK THAT'S MATERIALIZED UNTIL THEN. Buchsbaum has already played out a lot of fantasies. But with three years to go until his fiftieth birthday, one senses a desire to do more work on a larger scale, projects designed to attract large numbers of people without anybody having to say they're embarrassed of chartreuse.

So Buchsbaum will continue to push out into the frontiers of irony; he'll continue to draw from a whirling cultural grab bag for things to borrow, enhance, or scramble into a new order. Although not one to compare his work with that of others, one can't help but see the similarities between the architect and a certain client: occasionally, the act of designing the stage for human action is reminiscent of the act of creating on stage. SOMETIMES, YOU CAN'T IMAGINE HOW THE SAME MIND COULD PUT ALL THOSE PIECES TOGETHER AND COME UP WITH A PERSONALITY THAT'S ALWAYS BETTE MIDLER, EVEN IF SHE'S DOING SOMETHING YOU'VE NEVER SEEN HER DO BEFORE. SOMETIMES THE PIECES DON'T FIT THAT WELL. BUT SOMETIMES, AFTER SHE'S BROUGHT THE AUDIENCE THROUGH SO MANY CHANGES, THEY'RE THRILLED. And sometimes, she even makes them laugh and feel at ease.

An architect has to be an amateur psycho-analyst. People react to signs and symbols. I'm designing a store at the moment that proposes to sell rather expensive clothes. So I'm designing the place to *look* expensive. Which means the choice of certain woods, certain densities of color, and a definite richness of form are important. The irony lies in the fact that the space could be made to suggest something completely different, let's say austerity—yet cost as much, or maybe more. It's the manipulation of familiar imagery that evokes these reactions.

CHARIVARI MEN'S AND WOMEN'S STORES

New York, New York
1978

design	Design Coalition: Alan Buchsbaum with Stephen Tilly
	assisted by Charles Thanhauser
photography	Charles Nesbit
text	Frederic Schwartz

The inventive multilevel, mazelike plans of the Charivari Men's and Women's stores created spaces for in-store boutiques that were the first of their kind. Brass clothing racks and high-gloss ceilings, coupled with mirrors in expected and unexpected locations, offered a multi-material fashion statement for the very hip, which featured younger, more adventurous prêt-a-porter.

Both men's and women's stores were stimulating environments that encouraged exploration of merchandise on different levels and in a variety of high-interest niches. Posh, slick surfaces were contrasted to partially scraped, cast-iron columns, with capitals Buchsbaum highlighted in gold leaf. Blond wood casework with black marble countertops, designed in shapes to suit display and cashier functions, contributed additional variety to glittering store interiors. People came to shop, to watch, and to parade. It was "trend-setting on the cheap," recalls Stephen Tilly (who also remembers that Design Coalition's last payment was in clothing).

FILM FORUM 1

New York, New York
1981

design   Design Coalition: Stephen Tilly with Alan Buchsbaum
assisted by Charles Thanhauser
photography   Charles Nesbit
text   Frederic Schwartz

This Soho institution showing offbeat films and revivals was the first movie theater built in Lower Manhattan in decades. It has since been demolished. Instead of building a "black box," two theaters were inserted into the open space of a recycled commercial garage. A prominent marquee was added to the asymmetrical facade, and the existing openings were glazed with industrial window sashes to reflect the two screening rooms inside. The translucent screen window illuminated the narrow entrance space where patrons enjoyed a drink at the bar before the show. An exposed bowstring truss defined the lobby and structure of the building.

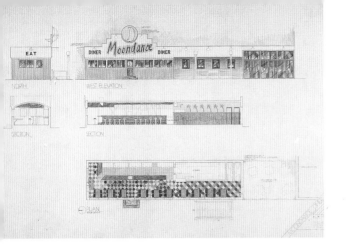

MOONDANCE DINER

New York, New York
1983

design	Alan Buchsbaum assisted by Davis Sprinkle
photography	Oberto Gili
text	Frederic Schwartz

In 1981, Larry Panish, a hot young Manhattan chef, bought the seventy-year-old Tunnel Diner on the edge of Soho. When Buchsbaum was asked to renovate it on a tight budget, he headed directly for the restaurant- and building-supply stores on the Bowery and Canal Street. His objective was to design a glitzy interior befitting the diner's new-wave menu and name.

Inspired by gas station signage, Buchsbaum designed a mechanically rotating, bright yellow back-lit half moon over the entry and also spelled out the name of the diner in the large shimmering sequins of car-wash signs. Inside, glittery gray-blue laminate was used to surface the tables, and the seating was upholstered in sparkling vinyl. The floor was refinished in a multicolor harlequin tile pattern. Theatrical spotlights and a midnight-blue ceiling reinforce the Moondance theme. Buchsbaum's seating, counter, and kitchen layout suggest a traditional diner, but he nevertheless achieved an alternative ambiance, which is felt immediately upon entry.

While the Moondance was the first of many diner "comebacks" in Manhattan, this was not a simplistic restoration. More than fifteen years after its completion, the Moondance remains a fresh, popular brunch and late-night spot where one is equally comfortable sipping coffee or chardonnay.

Among the thousands of New York actors, writers, composers, dancers, artists, and musicians working as waiters was Jonathan Larson (1961–1996), the 1996 Pulitzer Prize–winning dramatist and composer of the landmark rock opera *Rent*. For ten years, while perfecting his craft, Larson supported himself as a waiter at the Moondance.

GENNARO ANDREOZZI OFFICES

New York, New York
1982

design   Design Coalition: Alan Buchsbaum assisted by Thom O'Brien

photography   Norman McGrath

text   Frederic Schwartz

WHAT'S WRONG WITH THIS PICTURE? IT MAY LOOK THROWN TOGETHER, BUT IT'S REALLY VERY WORKED OUT. EVERYTHING DOESN'T HAVE TO HAVE A NAME.

The Chelsea offices of Gennaro Andreozzi, a television-commercial production company, were a riotous juxtaposition of ideas, materials, textures, and colors. This project illustrated Buchsbaum's attitude during this period in his career: anything goes, and everything can go together. Extensively published, this trendsetting design combined bold saturated colors with off-the-shelf elements, low-tech construction, and an ad-hoc selection and placement of furnishings.

The multilevel, 3,500-square-foot interior renovation deftly incorporated fabrics and furnishings more frequently found in the home. The wide variety of artifacts scattered throughout included a curving glass-block wall, antiques, a table with nine legs, a structural column painted in trompe l'oeil marble against a checkerboard background in slate and quarry tile, a found, multipaned wood-framed window, stadium seating, Bank of England chairs, velvet curtains, billboard and factory lights, exposed pipes, industrial fixtures, and a prefabricated greenhouse with rattan furniture.

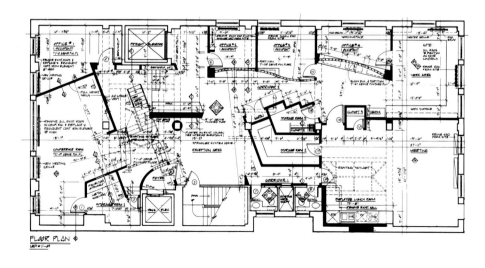

FLOOR PLAN

6-5-4-3-2-1 WYOMING

1982

design	Design Coalition: Alan Buchsbaum
mural design	Alan Buchsbaum, Donald Newman, and Rosalind Krauss
lighting consultant	Edward Effron Associates
photography	Peter Paige, courtesy Italian Tile Center
text	Frederic Schwartz

To demonstrate the beauty and adaptability of Italian tile, nineteen leading American designers were given free rein to illustrate their ideas in residential settings for Casa Tile '82, held in the Italian Trade Center in New York. Buchsbaum envisioned a rugged outland with a surreal quality. The tile field, set on an axis, appears suspended, while a mathematical pattern of mustards, mauves, ochers, and greens gives the terrain movement and cadence. A sweeping black-and-white photomural creates an abstract panorama and almost dizzying sense of height, so that the blue rattan chairs appear poised at the edge of a precipice somewhere near Wyoming. The scale and bold red of the shiny motorcycle activate this landscape and illustrate Buchsbaum's drama and caprice, and his interest in the surreal and theatrical productions.

IF THERE IS SUCH A THING AS PURE DESIGN, I DON'T KNOW WHAT IT IS. I NEED A PROBLEM, A CONTEXT. LIKE AN ACTOR, I HAVE TO CREATE A PROBLEM.

I WOULD RATHER NOT BE QUOTED AND LEAVE THE INTERPRETATION OF THIS ROOM TO THE VIEWER.

HEGEL'S VACATION
1984

design	Alan Buchsbaum assisted by Davis Sprinkle
lighting consultant	Magnan/Payne
table fabrication	Constantine Joannides
photography	Elliot Fine, courtesy Italian Tile Center
text	Frederic Schwartz

This installation, designed for Casa Tile '84, creates its own outdoors via clever use of Italian ceramic tiles and black-and-white photography. Buchsbaum used photography to provide the surface patterns for the draped chair, the wood-grained table laminate, and the cinematic view out the window. The stark black-and-white patterns were contrasted with the rich, polished terra-cotta tile, and the gray walls were painted to resemble plaster. The chipped tile pieces framing the window and door evoke a sense of incompleteness.

overleaf

RED
1983

design	Alan Buchsbaum assisted by Davis Sprinkle
photography	courtesy New York Magazine
text	Frederic Schwartz

This installation for a *New York Magazine* design story used red, a very traditional and royal color according to Buchsbaum, and industrial objects to prove that it is easy to move away from the neutrals and use a color that can be tricky. The red was tempered by the shadow of a lacy screen, hanging plants, and Jonathan Bonner's oxidized copper weathervane, which evoked a perpetual breeze. By combining objects of different scale and materiality, Buchsbaum proclaimed that a person would need a real sense of humor for this room.

PATRICOFF KITCHEN

New York, New York
1984

design — Alan Buchsbaum
photography — Norman McGrath
text — Frederic Schwartz

In response to the clients' request for a large, white, contemporary, and "glamorous" kitchen with two industrial-quality stoves, sinks, and dishwashers, Buchsbaum served up a sculptural masterpiece of whiteness and warmth. Explained Buchsbaum, IT'S BASICALLY A WHITE KITCHEN WITH SHAPES AND PATCHES OF MUTED COLORS. NEITHER THE BUILDING NOR THE APARTMENT WAS EQUIPPED TO ACCOMMODATE THE PLUMBING, ELECTRICITY, AND DUCTING THAT TODAY'S WELL-EQUIPPED KITCHEN REQUIRES. IN ADDITION, THERE WERE LOAD-BEARING COLUMNS THAT COULDN'T BE REMOVED WHEN WE COMBINED THE TWO ROOMS THAT WERE TO BE USED FOR THE ENLARGED KITCHEN. WE COULDN'T TURN THESE SPACES INTO ONE ORDINARY REC-TANGULAR ROOM.

Buchsbaum transformed these limitations into positive features. Irregular forms, the segmented arch in particular, were an important theme. The shapes were visible at the top of the cabinetry and shelving; cabinet door fronts did not match up. On the ceiling, the functional elements stood out in relief and were alternately smoothed, twisted, and exaggerated into sculpture. To mediate the sterility of an all-white kitchen further, Buchsbaum used accents of exotic woods, warm pink granite on the backsplash, counter, and tabletops, brass pulls, and several shades of Italian tile on the floor in an offbeat checkerboard pattern. The result was an extraordinary kitchen with masterful planning, classic whiteness, rich materials, exquisite details, and deliberate asymmetries that represent the softening of High-Tech.

KEATON APARTMENT

New York, New York
1982

design	Alan Buchsbaum assisted by Charles Thanhauser
photography	David Heinlein
text	Frederic Schwartz

Buchsbaum transformed Diane Keaton's Upper West Side apartment into a serene, unified, pared-down loft by using white paint, minimal detailing, and light, natural wood. His signature industrial light fixtures, simple and comfortable custom-designed furniture, and low-cost Bank of England chairs all worked together. Most notable was the elegant, rhythmic, built-in cabinet running the full length of the bedroom wall, an asymmetrical, modular composition of drawer faces and finger pulls. The countertop was set at window-sill height to establish a low, uniform datum line for the apartment.

BALABAN/GROSSMAN APARTMENT

New York, New York
1982

design   Alan Buchsbaum assisted by Davis Sprinkle
photography   Oberto Gili
text   Alan Buchsbaum

THIS APARTMENT IS IN THE APTHORP, AN EARLY-TWENTIETH-CENTURY ITALIANATE COURTYARD BUILDING ON THE UPPER WEST SIDE OF MANHATTAN. THE BUILDING HAS A VARIETY OF APARTMENTS THAT ARE MOSTLY PAINTED WHITE AND HAVE RETAINED THEIR ORIGINAL DETAILING, IN THIS CASE A BEAUTIFUL MOSAIC TILE FLOOR IN THE ENTRANCE. THE WALLS OF THE APARTMENT WERE PAINTED FLAT WHITE AND THE WOOD MOLDINGS HIGH GLOSS WHITE. THE LIGHTING IS LOW VOLTAGE, WHICH GIVES A WHITER LIGHT THAN STANDARD VOLTAGE. IN THESE SHARP WHITE ROOMS, THE NUANCES OF THE MANY IDIOSYNCRATIC FURNISHINGS ARE QUITE NOTICEABLE. THE OCCUPANTS OF THE APARTMENT ARE A SCREENWRITER, AN ACTOR, AND THEIR SEVEN-YEAR-OLD DAUGHTER. THEY HAVE A WONDERFUL SENSE OF HUMOR AND ARE VERY WELL INFORMED ABOUT DESIGN. THEY ENTERTAIN FREQUENTLY, AND MANY TIMES HAVE TWENTY OR MORE PEOPLE FOR DINNER. THE GATHERINGS ARE INFORMAL, AND GUESTS ARE ALLOWED TO BRING FRIENDS, SO THE RESULTING GROUPS CAN BECOME QUITE LARGE. FOR THIS REASON MANY TABLES (AND CHAIRS) WERE NEEDED, YET IT WOULD HAVE BEEN CUMBERSOME TO HAVE THEM IN OPEN VIEW. I RECOMMENDED A BUFFET IN THE ENTRY HALL. THIS TABLE IS MADE OF PLYWOOD COVERED WITH FORMICA COLORCORE, LEAVANTO ROSO MARBLE, AND SARDINIAN WHITE GRANITE. THE TOP RESTS ON FOUR CYLINDRICAL LEGS AND IS A PARALLELOGRAM IN PLAN. ALL OF THE FURNITURE IS ON CASTERS SO THAT IT CAN BE MOVED AT WILL.

THE BANQUETTE IN THE LIVING ROOM IS COVERED IN NATURAL LINEN CANVAS WITH REMOVABLE COVERS. CUSTOM-DESIGNED ADIRONDACK CHAIRS OF ASH WOOD HAVE PINK CANVAS CUSHIONS. THE CHAIRS ARE OVER-SCALED FOR COMFORT; THEY SIMULTANEOUSLY SCALE DOWN THE OTHER FURNISHINGS AND BALANCE THE BABY GRAND PIANO. THE BANK OF ENGLAND CHAIRS ARE PROSAIC OFFICE CHAIRS LACQUERED BLACK. THE CHAIRS ARE VERY COMFORTABLE AND HAVE A BEAUTIFUL SCULPTED FORM. A COFFEE TABLE MADE OF SARDINIAN GRAY GRANITE HAS SOME SMOOTH EDGES AND SOME ROUGH EDGES; IT RESTS ON ARBITRARILY PLACED COLUMNS AND TWO SLAB SUPPORTS COVERED IN FORMICA COLORCORE. THE DINING ROOM HAS A TABLE WITH A SARDINIAN PINK GRANITE TOP ON A BASE OF PLUMBER'S PIPE ON CASTERS. THE TABLE WAS MADE IN TWO SECTIONS SO THAT IT CAN BE PULLED APART FOR LARGE DINNER PARTIES. ANOTHER BUFFET, OF FORMICA COLORCORE ON RANDOMLY PLACED COLUMNS, HAS FOUR SECTIONS. ONE CAN BE USED AS AN EXTENSION OF THE GRANITE TABLE; THE OTHER THREE CAN BE COMBINED TO MAKE AN ADDITIONAL DINING TABLE.

BRINKLEY APARTMENT

New York, New York
1983

design	Alan Buchsbaum assisted by Tim Schollaert and Frank Schroder
photography	Langdon Clay
text	Frederic Schwartz

MY CLIENT, A WOMAN, TENDS TO WEAR THINGS LIKE FATIGUES AND LOOK FABULOUS. SO I TRIED TO MAKE HER APARTMENT REFLECT THAT. BASICALLY, I'D HOPED IT WOULD END UP LOOKING AS THOUGH IT HADN'T BEEN DESIGNED.

The interior design of Christie Brinkley's Upper West Side apartment was a study in minimalist, casual chic. Buchsbaum painted the walls and ceiling in different shades of white, added a hand-painted green and yellow frieze to the twenty-foot-high space, and stained the wood floor light gray. In the living area, he composed a simple still life: pink-chenille-upholstered La-Z-Boy, lavender slip-covered sofa, baby grand piano, custom-designed hearthside rug, and coffee table—the focal point. The tabletop was specified in three different stones, and its base, on casters, was surfaced in Formica ColorCore laminate. The table could be configured to serve different functions. As a touch of insouciant elegance, a Waterford crystal chandelier was hung in a corner.

BARKIN LOFT

New York, New York
1984

design   Alan Buchsbaum
drapery   Alan Buchsbaum and Mary Bright
photography   Oberto Gili
text   Alan Buchsbaum

I AM THE ARCHITECT OF THIS LOFT, AND ALTHOUGH IT MAY
SOUND FATUOUS TO SAY THAT DESIGNING IT AND BUILDING
IT WERE AN IMMENSE PLEASURE, THEY WERE. MUCH OF
THE EXCITEMENT CAME FROM WORKING WITH MY CLIENT,
AN AMERICAN ACTRESS, WHO ASKED ME TO "FIX" HER
PLACE IN CHELSEA. IT MAY ALSO SOUND FATUOUS TO SAY
THAT I LIKE MY CLIENTS, BUT I DO. THEY ARE PRIMARILY
ENTERTAINERS, AND AS THE WORD IMPLIES, THEY ARE
ENTERTAINING. THEY ARE ALSO ADVENTUROUS AND OPEN
TO NEW EXPERIENCES, SO THAT SUGGESTING THE UNTRIED
AND DARING IS MORE INTERESTING TO THEM THAN COPY-
ING A PREVIOUSLY REALIZED DESIGN. THIS PARTICULAR
ACTRESS WAS NOT A PARTICULARLY EASY CLIENT. SHE IS
CAPABLE OF EXPRESSING EVERYTHING AN ACTRESS MAY BE
ASKED TO EXPRESS, AND LIKES TO PRACTICE HER CRAFT. I
DON'T THINK WE COVERED VIOLENCE, BUT WE DID DO CRY-
ING, DEPRESSION, HATRED, AND PARANOIA, AS WELL AS
TRUST, LOVE, ENTHUSIASM, AND LAUGHING. WE DID A LOT
OF LAUGHING. SHE IS A VERY FUNNY WOMAN. SHE IS ALSO
VERY BEAUTIFUL AND VERY TOUGH. IT SHOULD BE OBVI-
OUS BY NOW THAT I AM HER FAN. THE FURNISHINGS ARE
SCATTERED IN THE AREAS WE DECIDED MIGHT BE THE
BEST PLACES TO SIT AND EAT. THERE ARE NO FORMAL
AXES, AND THE CHAIRS AND TABLES LOOK AS THOUGH
THEY WERE SET DOWN BY THE MOVERS AND MIGHT BE
MOVED TO SOME OTHER SPOT, SHOULD THE WHIM ARISE.
THE FURNISHINGS THEMSELVES ARE UNRELATED, EXCEPT
PERHAPS BY COLOR. THEY ARE MEANT TO CONVEY FEEL-
INGS OF COMFORT AND LACK OF PRETENSION. THE COLORS
OF THE LOFT ARE PURPOSELY INDECISIVE. THEY SLIDE IN
BOTH DIRECTIONS, TOWARD THE WARM AND THE COOL.
THE LOFT IS LIT BY FOUR TRACKS CONTROLLED FROM THE
ENTRY. THE VARIOUS ZONES OF THE LOFT—LIVING, DINING,
KITCHEN, SLEEPING—CAN, LIKE A STAGE SET, BE LIT OR
DARKENED ACCORDING TO THE FOCUS OF ATTENTION.

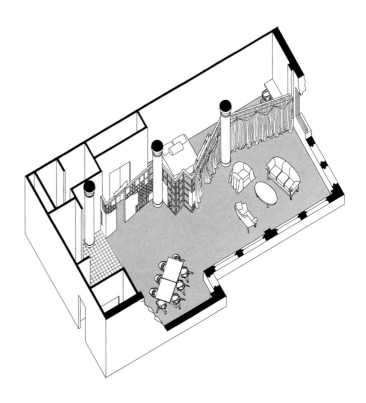

I DOUBT THIS LOFT WOULD HAVE EVER BEEN DONE IN THIS MANNER WERE MY CLIENT NOT THE PERSON SHE IS. SO I MUST CALL HER MY COLLABORATOR, EVEN THOUGH SHE KNOWS LITTLE OF ARCHITECTURE. SHE PROVIDED THE BASIC PROGRAM, WHICH WAS SIMPLE ENOUGH: A SEPARATION OF PRIVATE AREAS (SLEEPING, DRESSING, BATH, STUDY) FROM LIVING AREAS (LIVING, DINING, KITCHEN, ENTRY). SHE ALSO PROVIDED THE POETIC DESCRIPTION OF THE LESS DEFINABLE QUALITIES THE LOFT WAS TO POSSESS. I WOULD WRITE THEM NOW, COULD I JUST REMEMBER WHAT SHE SAID, BUT PERHAPS THE PICTURES WILL SUGGEST WHAT INFORMATION WAS IMPARTED. OUT OF THIS LIST, THE CONCEPT OF THE "WALL" WAS DEVISED. THE WALL, LIKE THE OWNER, EXHIBITS CONFLICTING DUALITIES: OPACITY AND TRANSLUCENCE, HARD AND SOFT, OPEN AND CLOSED. THE WALL ZIGS AROUND THE EXISTING CYLINDRICAL COLUMNS OF THE BUILDING. ON THE PRIVATE SIDE ARE RAW TIMBERS AND PLYWOOD STAINED A MILKY PINK. THE STRUCTURE OF THE WALL TOWARD THE EAST END OF THE LOFT IS COMPOSED OF A TIGHT GRID; TOWARD THE WEST END, THE GRID BECOMES LARGER AND THE TIMBERS THICKER. TWO PASSAGEWAYS THROUGH THE WALL ARE MARKED WITH HORIZONTAL FLOATING LINTELS. ON THE PUBLIC SIDE, THERE ARE SIX HUNDRED YARDS OF VOILE DRAPED VOLUPTUOUSLY; IT PLAYS WITH THE LIGHT PROJECTED FROM BOTH SIDES. NEED I SAY THAT THE ACTRESS IS VERY SEDUCTIVE?

MIDLER LOFT

New York, New York
1984

design   Design Coalition: Alan Buchsbaum with German Martinez
decorative painting   Nancy Kintish
photography   Oberto Gili
text   Alan Buchsbaum

BETTE MIDLER'S 4,500-SQUARE-FOOT LOFT IS IN AN 1891 LANDMARKED, DUTCH-GABLED WAREHOUSE IN TRIBECA WITH MAJESTIC VIEWS OF THE HUDSON RIVER. UNTIL RECENTLY THE HEAVY TIMBER AND BRICK BUILDINGS OF THE AREA WERE USED FOR LIGHT MANUFACTURING AND WAREHOUSING. THE RAW INTERIOR SPACES ARE GENERALLY LIGHT AND AIRY WITH HIGH CEILINGS, ROWS OF CAST-IRON COLUMNS, PAINTED-WOOD WINDOWS, AND RAW BRICK WALLS. THE PUBLIC AREAS OF THE LOFT WERE RESTORED TO THEIR NATURAL STATE. THE COLUMNS, BRICK WALLS, WINDOW FRAMES, PIPES AND VALVES, EXPOSED CEILING TIMBERS, AND WOOD FLOORS WERE CLEANED AND REFINISHED. THE "FLOATING" MUSIC STUDIO, WHICH IS SUPER-SOUNDPROOFED, AND THE BEDROOMS AND BATHS HAVE RAISED FLOORS, SHEETROCK WALLS, AND SUSPENDED CEILINGS THAT CONTAIN LIGHTING, AIR CONDITIONING, AND HEATING. THESE SPACES CONTRAST WITH THE EXISTING ARCHITECTURE AND INCORPORATE A VOCABULARY OF GLASS BLOCK, CARPET, CERAMIC TILE, MIRROR, MARBLE, AND PASTEL-PAINTED WALLS.

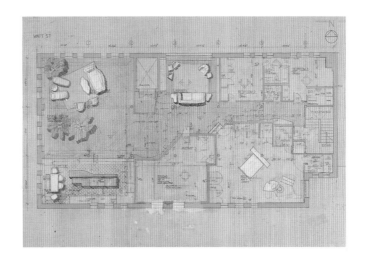

THE DIVINE ONE WAS INTERESTED IN ART NOUVEAU AND
ART DECO BUT PREFERRED THE DECORATION OF HER LOFT
TO HAVE THE FLAVOR OF THE WIENER WERKSTÄTTE AND
CHARLES RENNIE MACKINTOSH. I FOUND SOME THIRTIES
PIECES IN SOHO THAT I HAD REBUILT AND REUPHOLSTERED.
WE MET IN VIENNA WHERE WE BOUGHT TWO CHAIRS, TWO
MIRRORS, A SMALL TABLE BY JOSEF HOFFMANN, AND CIRCA-
1900 LIGHT FIXTURES FOR THE GUEST BATH. WHEREAS
THE AVERAGE PERSON MIGHT HAVE ONE OR TWO IDEAS
ABOUT AN ASPECT OF DESIGN, MIDLER WOULD HAVE 250,
ALL INTERESTING. I WOULD HAVE TO CHOOSE ONE AND
TURN IT INTO A REALITY. HER ACTIVE IMAGINATION WAS
MY BIGGEST CHALLENGE.

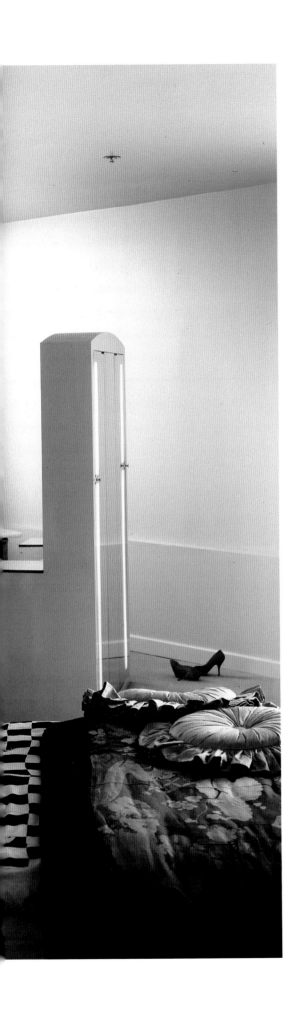

WINTOUR/SHAFFER TOWNHOUSE

New York, New York
1984

design   Alan Buchsbaum assisted by Davis Sprinkle
photography   Oberto Gili
text   Frederic Schwartz

Buchsbaum's renovation of this mid-nineteenth-century four-story Soho townhouse is spartan in its restraint and in its sophisticated combination of modernity and romance. Buchsbaum explained: THE PROJECT BECAME ONE OF CREATIVE PRESERVATION. WHILE MANY OF THE ORIGINAL DETAILS WERE SALVAGED, WE WERE NOT AIMING TOWARD A HISTORIC RESTORATION. IN A HOUSE OF THIS SIZE, ONE OR TWO STROKES SET THE TONE.

Privacy was important in the house's plan: two teen-age children live on the ground floor; the kitchen and dining areas are on the second floor; a living room and study occupy the third floor; and the master bedroom suite takes up the entire fourth floor. As ample open space was another priority, Buchsbaum cleared two floors of their walls. The supporting wall around the main stair was removed, and a thin, elegant steel column was added for structural support. The steel was left exposed to contrast with the carefully restored wooden banister and carved baseboards. A pair of original pilasters were fashioned into freestanding columns to delineate the dining area. Each piece of furniture, mostly of nineteenth-century origin, takes on a minimalist, sculptural presence against the off-white tones of the restored walls and patterned textiles. The only architectural elements other than the steel stair support are sandblasted glass doors, which close off the study without blocking daylight, and a wall of wooden bookshelves.

THERE IS AN ABSENCE OF DESIGN RATHER THAN A STRONG PRESENCE.

JOEL/BRINKLEY PENTHOUSE

New York, New York
1985

design	Alan Buchsbaum assisted by David Culmer Skelley and Corey Delany
photography	Oberto Gili
text	Corey Delany

For their "uptown pad," on Central Park West, rock star Billy Joel and supermodel Christie Brinkley wanted the casual downtown loft that Buchsbaum had become well known for designing. The 2,500-square-foot penthouse required a complete renovation, extensive structural work, and the installation of state-of-the-art sound and mechanical systems.

Guests emerge from the elevator into a cool, almost watery, glass-block entry and then progress to a space of tinted pastel walls that accentuate the special quality of light found high above the shadows of the city. The experience parallels that of a diver rising from the green depths of the ocean to the surface. Terraces on all four sides and a greenhouse highlight the spectacular views of Central Park and midtown skyscrapers.

Discrete suites contain the private areas, and a diagonally organized open plan accommodates eating, living, and entertaining. Large-scale, custom-designed cabinetry and voluptuously curved furniture, in eye-popping colors and unexpected fabrics, anchor the floating golden penthouse high above the city.

Buchsbaum's own designs are scattered throughout, including the Pencilmarkings rug, Wintour Table, an Aalto-esque bookcase, and a dining table made from slabs of rock-cut marble. These elements are mixed with his signature use of Bank of England chairs, Italian light fixtures, and other commercial components. The inherent beauty of the mechanics of the fireplace, a freestanding object, is celebrated. A complex, big, bold, blue storage wall designed for the sound system and record collection marries function with aesthetics. The red Rock Star Coffee Table is set against an extravagant custom sofa in blue velvet with Cadillac-fin arms.

The older I get, the more impatient I become with polite conversation. I always find myself wanting to open with some insulting question like "How much did that cost?" or "Is the rumor I hear about you true?" The last thing I'm interested in is a living room that is going to promote polite banality.

As Martin Filler wrote: "Buchsbaum was the ideal interior designer. His schemes were invariably practical, extraordinarily comfortable, and ingeniously adaptable, stylish but unpretentious and advanced but easily livable. He managed the difficult trick of creating spaces that were absolutely up-to-the-minute without seeming trendy or ephemeral, though he would be the last one to say that he was designing for the ages. That sense of authentic immediacy gives his designs the rare ability to define and epitomize a given moment simultaneously, and will no doubt contribute to his work of the eighties being viewed in retrospect as among the most focused in a period of considerable confusion."

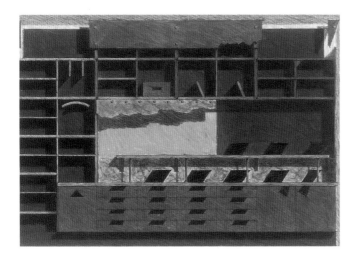

CENTRAL PARK

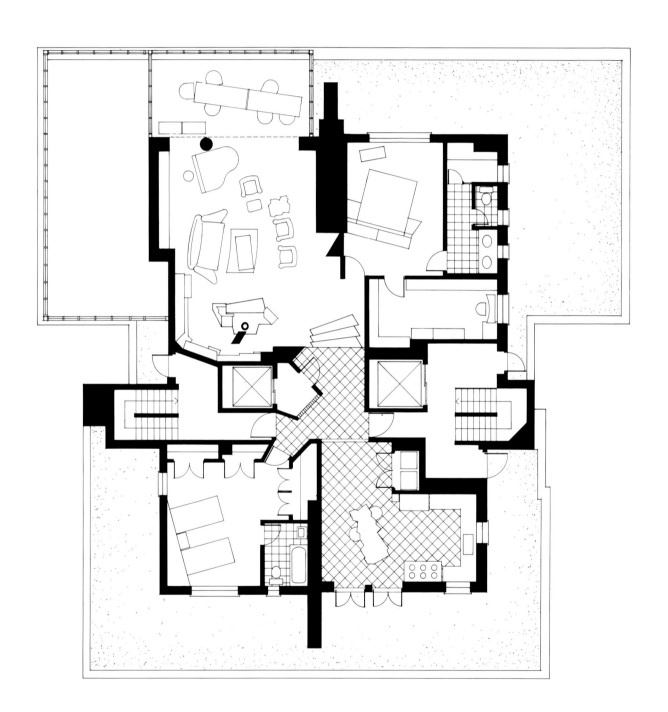

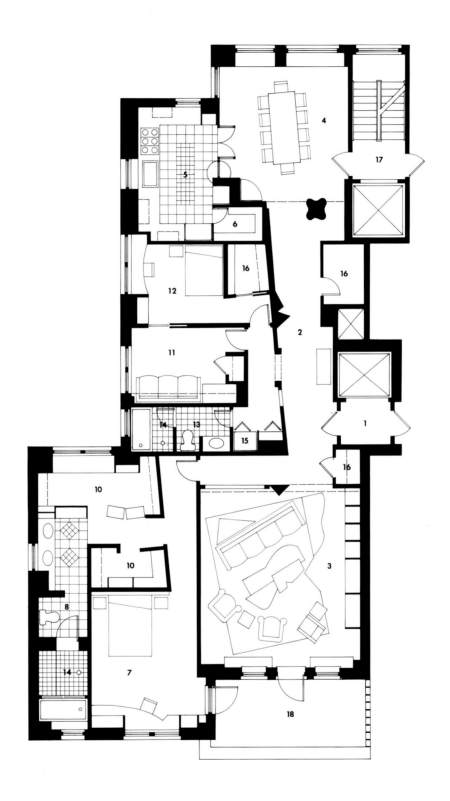

GRAMERCY PARK

DENNIS APARTMENT

New York, New York
1986

design   Alan Buchsbaum with Jaime Vasquez and Corey Delany
associated architect   Frederic Schwartz, Anderson/Schwartz Architects
photography   Michael Mundy
text   Frederic Schwartz

Buchsbaum's last residential design in Manhattan, the Dennis Apartment, overlooking Gramercy Park, was the epitome of eighties urban elegance and sophistication. The clients felt that the apartment, though large, was dark and claustrophobic. Buchsbaum gutted the space, creating a generous entry with views across the apartment—from the dining room across the hall into the living room and back—and also outside to the park and skyline. The more private activities of the program were hidden behind this layer—master bedroom suite, children's/guest quarters, kitchen.

Exceptional architectural, lighting, and decorating details were carefully located throughout the apartment. The serene palette—accents of cobalt, melon, and sage against white—highlighted the rich variety of textures and materials—fabrics, woods, stones, metals. A large-scale blue plaster quatrefoil column anchored the dining room; an ebonized-ash wall cabinet for books, television, recording equipment, and objects set the tone for the living room. The kitchen was a disciplined study in black and white; warm touches included mirrored wood cabinets floating on the walls.

WINTOUR TABLE
1985

design	Alan Buchsbaum
production	Ecart International
photography	courtesy Ecart International
text	Frederic Schwartz

Buchsbaum was asked by Andrée Putman to design a dining table for her company, Ecart. He delivered the elegant Wintour Table, named in honor of his friend Anna. Its wood frame and its legs, set on the diagonal, were of ebonized mahogany; its top was an elegant, sandblasted, lacquered sheet of steel. Buchsbaum contrasted natural and industrial materials in a minimalist composition that offered a touch of modern sophistication—at its corners, the table cleverly demonstrated a gap between its thin, floating top and its sturdy, shapely legs.

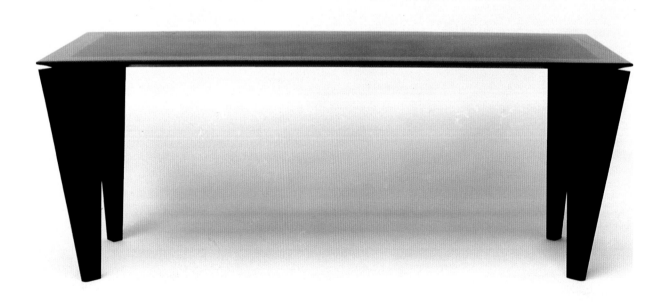

NEVELE CHAIR
1986

design	Alan Buchsbaum and Marc L´Italien
production	Dennis Miller Associates
photography	Steve Moore
text	Frederic Schwartz

The Nevele Hotel in the Catskill Mountains requested strong new chairs for their lobby that would meet the demands of the "borscht belt" resort. Buchsbaum and L'Italien produced this caricature of the great club chairs of the thirties and forties in bold red with enormous upholstered arms that leap forward as an invitation to comfort.

SUGAR CHAIR
1985

design	Alan Buchsbaum assisted by Jaime Vasquez
production	Dennis Miller Associates
photography	Steve Moore
text	Frederic Schwartz

The classic French club chair was stylized and its scale enlarged and reinterpreted by Buchsbaum. The chair is 38 inches wide, 32 inches deep, and 35 inches high with a 17-inch seat. An even larger prototype in dark green leather with stained maple feet was designed for the Dennis Apartment.

ROCK STAR COFFEE TABLE
1985

design	Alan Buchsbaum assisted by Jaime Vasquez
production	Dennis Miller Associates
photography	Steve Moore
text	Frederic Schwartz

Originally designed for Billy Joel and Christie Brinkley, the Rock Star Coffee Table includes a pull-out extension for drinks and snacks and a fixed lower shelf for books and magazines. The finish is bright red ColorCore plastic laminate on a plywood substrate with painted steel legs to match. The table is 50 inches long, 28 inches wide, and 21 inches high.

ELKES TABLES
1985

design	Alan Buchsbaum
table fabrication	Constantine Joannides
photography	Steve Moore
text	Frederic Schwartz

The Elkes dining and side tables, designed for a house in Rye, New York, exhibit a study of the visual and structural nature of the diagonal. The wood table bases are joined with sturdy pyramidal forms, trusses, and corner supports. The dining table has a rose granite top that contrasts with the fine finish of its pedestal; the side table is completely made of joined wood members.

O'KEEFE TOWNHOUSE

New York, New York
1986

design   Alan Buchsbaum and Marc L'Italien
                                         assisted by Corey Delany
associated architect   Frederic Schwartz, Anderson/Schwartz Architects
photography   Peter Aaron/ESTO
text   Marc L'Italien

This project for the actor Michael O'Keefe transformed the rooms of the parlor level of a narrow Greek Revival townhouse in Chelsea to loftlike living. The intent was to break down the cellular disposition of the original plan into one big, open area accommodating the functions of living, cooking, dining, and storage. The east wall-as-ruin was transformed into a vibrant, versatile, dense, multicolored storage unit to accommodate the actor's books, recording equipment, clothes, and collectibles. This wall also frames the entry, stairs, a closet, and an opening to a small galley kitchen. The entire length of the opposite wall was left untouched, in stark contrast to the storage wall, suggesting an increase in the size and scale of the room.

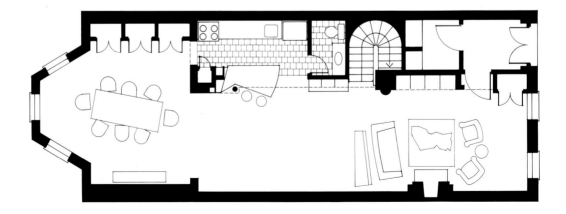

A HOUSE NEEDS ENOUGH PERMANENT OBJECTS SO THE INHABITANTS DON'T
BECOME DISORIENTED. BUT THAT DOESN'T MEAN IT CAN NEVER CHANGE.
DOES IT DISORIENT YOU IF YOUR FRIEND CHANGES HIS CLOTHES?

ALAN BUCHSBAUM, 1935–1987

from the *Village Voice,* 1987

Michael Sorkin

Alan Buchsbaum died on April 10, a casualty of AIDS. His third hospitalization lasted less than a week. Although many friends had allowed themselves to be lulled by the frail straws of new antibiotics and evanescent improvements in his condition, Alan knew it was the end and faced death with a sad equanimity.

While his hospital room was better than most, Alan's presence was a constant rebuke to its shortcomings. Gravely ill, though, he surrendered to the therapeutic oppression of its hygienic modernism. I don't know how much strength the clinical austerity of the place sapped from Alan, but being there must have been a special trial. Alan read environments immediately and with nuance, adeptly understood their mentalities, and responded directly. He loved artful, comfortable spaces and designed them better than anyone I know. How terrible his last days were in an environment of little art and less comfort. He'd wanted to die in his beautiful loft but ebbed too fast.

In many ways Alan Buchsbaum's architectural career was dedicated to redressing the deprivations of places like modern hospitals. Educated at Georgia Tech and MIT in the late fifties and early sixties—at the height of modernism's bloodless self-confidence—he came to New York and began work conventionally, spending five years as a designer in a succession of offices. Ending his apprenticeship, he embarked on a *Wanderjahr,* mostly in Italy and Japan. The impact was indelible. It's not so much that the journey was transformative, overwhelming in its revelations. Rather, it was a passage of corroboration, a visit to places where settings of conviviality and daily life had reached states of architectural perfection, where the arts and rituals of comfort were set out with fascinating grace and exquisite detail. Raised in Savannah, Georgia, Alan had come early to such scenes of civility and had them always in mind.

The ocean liner, another influence, is one of modern architecture's great metaphors, functionalism par excellence. The appeal is of beauty at once innocent and elaborate, an overwhelming aesthetic derived mechanistically from the pure exigencies of use. This is vulgar functionalism. Its discourse justifies motif-lifting at best and an architecture of constraint—the efficient drear of that hospital room—at worst. But Alan, a modern to his toes, was also a child of that irresistible liner. His lineage, however, descended from a somewhat different set of images and possibilities. Alan wouldn't have been mesmerized by ships' power and vastness or even by their particular vocabulary of shapes, the gross heroics of modernity. Rather, he'd have been enthralled by the careful craft of their tight problems of space and materials. He'd have adored their glamour. Alan was crazy about atmosphere.

In 1967, Alan set up practice with two friends, calling it the Design Coalition, a classic sixties moniker. The early work was much of its time: graphic, whimsical, exuberant. A hairdresser and men's clothing shop in Great Neck, constructed in 1969 on a bare-bones budget, iconographizes super-graphic profiles—a real head shop. The publication history of the project is revealing and typical: German, Japanese, and English architectural magazines; a New York newspaper; and *Ameruka,* a USIA effort directed at propagandizing the Poles—Alan's favorite. The point is the broadness. Alan was always well published, snapped up with equal relish by specialist journals, shelter magazines, and daily papers—not for any flacking or self-promotion but because of the work: from the first sophisticated yet accessible, artistic, and comfortable.

Indeed, Alan, in time, developed into an apostle of comfort, famously accommodating. It wasn't simply that his residential work was so livable, so unconstraining. Alan's spaces are always inviting, the kinds of spaces that virtually invite flopping onto the couch or taking a long, luxurious bath. Alan designed places to be in, not to stare at. The kind of comfort I'm trying to describe, though, is more about attitude than artifact. Alan was an architect who genuinely believed in program, in architecture's creative location in the terrain of desire. He had a seismographic sense of his clients' needs, quirks, and aspirations, and a willingness to go to considerable lengths to satisfy them. In a loft for Ellen Barkin, for example, this extended to hundreds of yards of voile, festooned with theatrical abandon in lieu of rigid walls: an actress's dream.

Alan's early reputation as a real originator centered on the invention of so-called High-Tech style. One thinks, for instance, of his own 1976 loft in which he composed a bedroom wall of an undulating plane of glass blocks and lit it with a row of blue runway lights. It's an incredibly memorable image, resonant and influential, very much of its moment. The point about High-Tech, however, is that it really isn't, particularly. What's being described is more of an off-the-shelf attitude, a willingness to engage frankly the lexicon of ready-made materials and the inevitable late-twentieth-century landscape of appliances. And, without question, this possibility began to be most mightily engaged with the rise of loft living in Manhattan. A better name for the High-Tech Alan pioneered might simply be Canal Street (its literal source) or, better still, Downtown.

Alan Buchsbaum was a leader in interpreting and organizing the collective epiphany that resulted from the great move to Lower Manhattan. It was as if a sensibility and a moment were destined for each other. Not that Alan was just a postmodern bricoleur, craftily accumulating; he was a designer, a real creator. The elements of the broader Downtown style were quickly established. Building on the cheap and on one's own familiarized a generation with the demands and possibilities of studs and sheetrock and with an aesthetic of incompletion and rearrangement. The use of lofts as both living and work spaces also interrupted the standard notions of the deployment of the elements of home. Instead of the cellular model, the loft generated an architecture of archipelago, a spray of islands of symbol and use. For architects, working in loft spaces retrieved one of modernism's most cherished possibilities, the free plan, excluded from the repetitive requirements of traditional urban dwellings. People would live differently here.

This possibility was enabled not simply by the spaces available but also by their new inhabitants. The idea of "alternative lifestyles" is surely overworked, but it is just as surely the historic purview of artists, the population that first liberated lofts for living. And the message of the crucible sixties—so important to Alan and his client generation—was certainly that the possibility of living with artistic latitude was a necessity and not a privilege. Alan's work was a continuous explication of this opening, an account of the joyous merger of the personal and the physical, a way of creating satisfying yet malleable wholes from impossibly disparate materials. In all of his designs, things sit comfortably together, like guests at a perfect dinner party. And Alan (who once wrote restaurant reviews under the pseudonym "FAT") loved dinner parties. He liked being spectator and participant at that happy symbiosis of pleasure and necessity, always watching for the moment when food, conversation, furnishings, lighting melded into what was, for him, the supremely architectural moment.

In an interview once, Alan remarked that he liked things that were a little bit off. It's a fine description of an important aspect of his work, the idea of difference short of dissonance. And it catches the kind of laid-back, modest, self-description that Alan—who had no patience for the posturing and polemic of the architectural salon—was inclined to. "A little bit off" is the natural condition of the spaces where Alan worked. Intervening in the city's old buildings means never confronting anything plumb, always dealing with spaces askew. Never mind the nice portrait of culture, the phrase surely locates the architect's task of reconciliation, both of the order of things—the harmonizing of stereos, Cuisinarts, family portraits, and Barbara Krugers—and the order of personalities—the inhabitants and the designers. Alan was a genius at exploring this territory between certainties, whether in his amazingly fresh color choices, his beautiful juxtapositions of unexpected shapes and textures, or his creation of utter felicity from improbable diversity.

In an early project, Alan (always a wizard at cabinetwork) designed a storage system supported on springs to compensate for the unevenness of a floor. This was a real "high-tech" approach, the imposition of an ideal solution on a resistant reality. He soon grew beyond this sort of response, inventing a style both considered and relaxed that was all his own. Alan freed objects—High-Tech, historic, funky—from the trammels of received wisdom about their ethics and use, reemploying them with marvelous originality. In his drawings, furniture, and rugs and in his architecture, there was always richness without excess and precision without parsimony. Alan created a body of work that will endure not only as a preeminent emblem of our moment but as an abiding inspiration to the world of design. Alan Buchsbaum was an extraordinary ornament to downtown, to New York, to architects, a presence of rare vitality. How we will miss him. But how he'll live on.

PEOPLE MIGHT FIND CURIOUS ELEMENTS IN MY WORK. I DON'T KNOW WHY, BECAUSE EVERYTHING DOES NOT LOOK CURIOUS OR UNUSUAL TO ME. I DO NOT HAVE A RIGID STYLE; I AM SAYING THAT I AM HAPPY THAT LOTS OF THINGS APPEAL TO ME—THAT I CAN ADAPT.

I'VE NEVER DESIGNED A PROJECT WHERE I DIDN'T DO THE WHOLE THING.

ECCO SHOES

New York, New York
1985

design	Alan Buchsbaum and Jaime Vasquez
	assisted by Corey Delany
lighting consultant	Clark Johnson
photography	Elliott Kaufman
text	Frederic Schwartz

Buchsbaum's last commercial design was a tour de force of bold colors, refined materials, and minimal design. Ecco began as a relatively simple renovation (two shops in Chelsea were to be combined into a 1,400-square-foot shoe store), which became extremely complicated once demolition started. A steel column filled with pipes was discovered between the shops, preventing the design of a central entry; Buchsbaum exaggerated the column, clad it in baked-enamel green-metal panels, and placed the recessed entry immediately to its right.

A strong diagonal, generated by the off-center entry, organized the plan. The diagonal was expressed by a ceiling soffit (used for lighting and the HVAC system), by the linear placement of the seating, and by its termination at the cashier's desk. A grid of salmon-colored floor tiles contrasted with soft, moss-green carpeting, mirrored pilasters, and truncated display fixtures. Two simple concepts completed the renovation: transparency, articulated by the sophisticated, seamless detailing of the storefront and glass shelving, and an airy interior painted minty green. Buchsbaum noted that the color was an attraction to shoppers and, in his usual offhand manner, remarked: IT'S A PERSONAL REFERENCE TO STAR TREK.

NEVELE HOTEL LOBBY

Ellenville, New York
1986

design	Alan Buchsbaum and Marc L'Italien
	assisted by Corey Delany
associated architect	Frederic Schwartz, Anderson/Schwartz Architects
photography	Elliott Kaufman
text	Marc L'Italien

TO PUT IT SIMPLISTICALLY, I WOULD SAY WE ARE IN A TRANSITION FROM THE "DESIGN IS GOOD FOR YOU" ERA TO "DESIGN IS FUN."

The Nevele Hotel, located in the Catskill Mountain resort area, has undergone a number of additions and interior renovations. The predominant style of these changes follows the 1953 design of Herbert Phillips, a former associate in the office of Morris Lapidus.

Buchsbaum's scheme for a new lobby was in the fifties style of the hotel. The large, amorphous, and irregularly shaped 10,000-square-foot space is anchored by dramatically lit, over-scaled, turquoise plaster quatrefoil columns that provide a foreground for a grand new registration desk. The scale and sinuous form of the desk create a stage set for arriving visitors as well as extensive work surfaces for the staff. Its back-lit brass fascia sparkles with the ambiance of the perforated-brass lighting fixtures of the period.

Bold custom-designed furniture and new wall-to-wall carpeting in a lively design, inspired by a Kandinsky painting, unify the lobby. Lighting fixtures, ornament, signage, and fountains were restored to maintain a historical link with the Nevele's past. Bright colors, plush furniture, new mirrors, and undulating forms recall the optimistic spirit of postwar interior design.

Smoke
Shop

V'SOSKE RUGS

1984–1987

design	Alan Buchsbaum
production	V'Soske
photography	courtesy V'Soske
text	Frederic Schwartz

Buchsbaum designed a series of rugs produced by V'Soske that are now in private and museum collections. He worked closely with the company to realize his designs through new developments in materials, techniques, weaves, dyes, and tufting. Ellen Hertzmarker and Roger McDonald write of their work with Buchsbaum:

"All of the work at V'Soske is collaborative and every collaboration is unique. Each architect or artist works in his or her own way, and it is up to us to listen and catch the intention. It is our goal and responsibility to keep the intention alive and intact. At our first meeting with Alan, he eyed us warily, but as we got to know each other, we developed a verbal shorthand. What was unique about Alan was the instinctive clarity of his intention. Each of the rugs was predicated on a different medium, the jumping-off point for interpretation of the rug.

"The choices in original medium were key in terms of the types of yarn and textures selected for their refractive or absorbing characteristics. The progression of the rugs expresses the development that was taking place in Alan's work; each rug became richer, denser, and more layered."

1985   *PILLOW RUG (HEARTH RUG)*

This rug was developed from a simpler version first designed for the Brinkley apartment. "Pillow Rug" suggests a comfortable resting place for a reclining figure. The head rests on a densely contoured, tufted gray-blue silk-and-worsted-wool pillow; the body, on the main area—a sheared, royal-blue-and-black form. Envisioned as a rug to be placed in front of a fireplace, it has irregular, "burned" edges.

PENCILMARKINGS

This rug developed from Buchsbaum's freehand sketch of graphite moving diagonally across yellow tracing paper. V'Soske developed various weights of yarn, methods of tufting that followed the energy of the strokes of Buchsbaum's hand, and new dying techniques to balance the color and vibration between the light and dark areas.

"Serious Leaves" was derived from a greatly enlarged photograph taken by Buchsbaum. V'Soske executed the design in a tight, flat texture with a remarkable range of black, white, and gray wools. The result is a richly detailed and subtle pattern that evokes the grain and depth of the original image.

1986   *FOR IMOGEN*

This rug was inspired by Buchsbaum's interest in the photographer Imogen Cunningham. The subject started as a photographic close-up of the center of a flower transformed through the medium of watercolor; it was further transformed into a soft, tactile rug for the floor or wall. Interpreted in varying weights of cut-pile wool yarn, the light areas appear as a shock on the blackened green field. The sensual element of Cunningham's work is echoed in the design.

Buchsbaum viewed his last project, completed two weeks before his death, as the completion of his series of rugs. He created a natural collage of hundreds of rose petals scattered on a black floor; Charles Nesbit photographed it from above (opposite). The scattered stigmas of the roses are executed in cut-pile silk to bring light into the composition. The square field of silk and wool tufted in a subtle grid grounds the base and allows the petals to float above the surface. Each petal, subtly detailed in color and shape, appears to be in constant motion. Beautiful detailed, highly romantic, and exuberant, "Rosie's Roses" (detail below) is a tour de force of craftsmanship and concept.

ALAN BUCHSBAUM
Personal Recollections

Steven Holl

When I first arrived in New York City during the extremely cold winter of 1977, I knew only one person in this dense mass of millions, my brother James, who was completing his Master of Fine Arts at Columbia University. The city was coated in layers of ice and I remember feeling the coldness of the frozen Hudson in my bones. I met an architectural student, Helen, whom I asked for help and direction in negotiating my way in New York. Helen suggested I call Alan Buchsbaum—not only a talented New York City architect but also a very giving person.

I remember the afternoon visit to Alan's Soho studio and his amazing graciousness and enthusiastic advice about working in Manhattan. He showed me the special blue runway lights he was using in his loft and his eyes sparkled with enthusiasm. He was a man excited by his work. I was amazed and amused; the orthodox cliché of selfish and mean-spirited New Yorkers found a paradox in this man, who could give an afternoon of advice to a complete stranger.

The time pressures and the distances of Manhattan blunted our encounters over the years. The city has a way of zigzagging friendships, of promoting only chance encounters, sometimes just once a year.

In 1985, Alan called me to say that he was giving himself a fiftieth birthday present: a trip to Kathmandu. After a flight from the Orient, he would be landing in Seattle the day after Christmas. That day was a long, dark, rainy one, typical of Seattle in the winter. The high tide outside the wooden cabin brought a blue-gray ocean horizon beside our wood fire. The fog was so heavy in the distance that the view of Seattle was gone. In its place was a blank, infinite ocean.

When Alan arrived we sat by the fire and talked about life, while our wooden rocking chairs, partially broken and strapped together with wire, creaked back and forth. Alan told me of his wanderings in Kathmandu and of the polychrome and rough-edged vernacular experiences. The melancholy of the afternoon weather was brightened by the yellow-glassy glow of the wet bark fire. I showed Alan the stone fireplace my father had built, each round stone picked from the beach, selected for its oblong flatness. On the beach, we found a few examples and skipped them into the rain-dotted bay.

I felt a curious and unspoken finality in Alan's stories, but I did not understand why. Months later, I got a call telling me "Alan died today," and I remember the sinking feeling of helplessness, a feeling that fills the empty moment of announcement as some here and now is hurtled away. My mind returned to the rainy December afternoon, the philosophical discussions supplemented by stick sketches in wet sand. Over the years I've felt the loss of a whole generation of many of the best souls in these short, collapsing decades—a slow far-striding silence. The frozen Hudson last winter reminded me of how a cold Manhattan was first brightened by the enthusiasm and warmth of Alan Buchsbaum, whose absence I will always feel.

Buchsbaum Loft 1, 1976

PROJECT LIST

This is the most complete list of all of the interiors, renovations, buildings, exhibitions, installations, furniture, rugs, products, and projects designed by Alan Buchsbaum and Design Coalition. The year indicates the first date of a sketch or drawing found in Buchsbaum's archives; the year indicated in the full project presentation is the year of completion. Within each year the projects are organized alphabetically. *Project* refers to those designs not built. Entries marked with an asterisk * are featured in the book.

1967

* "Barroon," inflatable vinyl hassock, for Beylerian Scott House, location unknown

1968

* Paper Poppy, paper goods store interiors, Inwood, New York, New York

  Kearney's Delicatessen, check-out counter, Upper West Side, New York, New York

1969

Lucidity, Inc., plastics store interiors, Upper East Side, New York, New York

* Metamorphosis, Ltd., hair salon interiors, Great Neck, New York

* CADO Furniture Corp., showroom interiors, Los Angeles, California

  CADO Furniture Corp., showroom interiors, Boston, Massachusetts

  CADO Furniture Corp., showroom interiors, Chicago, Illinois

* Gerber House, Chappaqua, New York

* Rosenberg House, Rome, Maine

1970

Jaffee Apartment, New York, New York

Thinking People, store interiors, Stamford, Connecticut

Thinking People, store interiors, Queens, New York

1971

* Bathroom, for *House Beautiful,* installation for article, New York, New York

  Bloch Apartment, interior renovation, Upper East Side, New York, New York

* Lloyds Apartment, interior renovation & furniture, Upper East Side, New York, New York

  Model Townhouse, renovation, Brooklyn, New York

1972

Bloch House Addition, *project,* location unknown

* Foam Furniture

  Gerber Apartment, interior renovation, New York, New York

* Here Comes Tomorrow, for Owens-Corning Fiberglas Corp., exhibition, New York, New York

* Lewin Apartment, New York, New York

* Tenenbaum Townhouse, interior design, furniture, & wallpaper, Savannah, Georgia

1973

* Cohen House, interior renovation & furniture, Kendall, Florida

* Haas Apartment, interior renovation & furniture, Upper East Side, New York, New York

1974

Binder Apartment, interior renovation & furniture, Upper East Side, New York, New York

Esther Gerber House, nursing home, *project,* Lakewood, New Jersey

Freund House, *project,* Southold, New York

Leisure Learning Center, Charlotte, North Carolina

Leisure Learning Center, El Paso, Texas

Semel, Petrusky and Buchsbaum Law Office, *project,* Financial District, New York, New York

Soladar House, interior renovation, Great Neck, New York

Stein Apartment, *project,* Upper West Side, New York, New York

Weiser Apartment, interior renovation, Upper West Side, New York, New York

1975

Bergman Apartment, interior renovation, *project,* Upper West Side, New York, New York

* Buchsbaum Loft 1, interior renovation & furniture, Soho, New York, New York

  Karp/Lebenson Loft, interior renovation, Soho, New York, New York

* Krauss Loft, interior renovation, Soho, New York, New York

  Lattman Apartment, interior renovation & furniture, *project,* Upper East Side, New York, New York

  Leslie House, addition & interiors, Woodmere, New York

  Pranx Office, interiors, *project,* Midtown, New York, New York

  Morris House, renovation, Gardner, New York

  Morris Studio, Gardner, New York

  Shuser Kitchen, New York, New York

1976

Acquire Magazine, office interiors & furniture, Midtown, New York, New York

Brinkley Apartment, interior renovation, Upper West Side, New York, New York

Carallain Apartment, interior renovation, *project,* College Point, New York, New York

Charivari, clothing store interiors, Riverside Square, New Jersey

Formica Exhibition, Louisville, Kentucky

Gold Apartment, interiors & furniture, Upper West Side, New York, New York

Hermanson Apartment, interior renovation & furniture, Upper East Side, New York, New York

Laserteque Disco, *project,* Upper East Side, New York, New York

Marantz Apartment, interior renovation, New York, New York

Poris Kitchen, interior renovation, *project,* New York, New York

Schecter Kitchen, interior renovation, Great Neck, New York

Schecter/Horowitz Apartment, interior renovation, *project,* Upper West Side, New York, New York

Tenenbaum House 1, *project,* Richmond County, South Carolina

Wahl Apartment, interior renovation, Upper East Side, New York, New York

1977

Carajohn Apartment, interior renovation, *project,* Upper East Side, New York, New York

Center Townhouse, addition, interior renovation, furniture & garden design, Savannah, Georgia

Cunningham & Walsh, telephone desk, New York, New York

* Miller Kitchen, interior renovation, Upper West Side, New York, New York

* The Play Setting, playground design, *project,* New Rochelle, New York

Schuman/Neal Office, *project,* Greenville, New York

Tenenbaum House 2, *project,* Richmond County, South Carolina

Wahl Apartment, interior renovation, New York, New York

1978

Boal Apartment, interior renovation, Greenwich Village, New York, New York

Brant Kitchen, interior renovation, Upper East Side, New York, New York

Bryskin Bath, interior renovation, Upper East Side, New York, New York

Donovan Apartment, interior renovation, New York, New York

* Charivari Men's and Women's store, clothing store interiors, Upper West Side, New York, New York

Charivari Men's store, clothing store interiors, Upper West Side, New York, New York

* Restivo Apartment, interior renovation, Greenwich Village, New York, New York

Reinhard Residence, interior renovation & furniture design, Forest Hills, Queens, New York

Rosenthal China, office interiors, *project,* Upper East Side, New York, New York

* Sanjurjo Penthouse, interior renovation & greenhouse, Greenwich Village, New York, New York

* Tenenbaum House, Columbia, South Carolina

Brant Kitchen, interior renovation, New York, New York

1979

* Abramson House, interior renovation, furniture, & wallpaper, Camotop, Maryland

Apple Table, for Knoll International, *project*

Boal Apartment, interior renovation, *project,* Greenwich Village, New York, New York

Charivari, clothing store renovation, Upper West Side, New York, New York

* Gerber/Rothberg Apartment, interior renovation & furniture, Upper West Side, New York, New York

* Hirsch Kitchen, interior renovation, New York, New York

Katz House, addition & interior renovation, Livingston, New Jersey

* Keaton Apartment, interior renovation & furniture, Upper West Side, New York, New York

Pagliuso Loft, interior renovation, *project,* New York, New York

Electroport, Pan Am Terminal, JFK Airport, Queens, New York

Restivo Apartment, interior renovation, Upper East Side, New York, New York

Rosenthal Apartment, interior renovation, *project,* New York, New York

Roth Cabinets, New York, New York

Shearer Apartment, interior renovation & addition, Upper West Side, New York, New York

1980

Borg Loft, interior renovation, *project,* New York, New York

Cooper, Dennis and Hirsch, office space planning, *project,* Midtown, New York, New York

Delaney Kitchen, interior renovation, Upper East Side, New York, New York

* Jakobson Bedroom, interior renovation & furniture, Upper East Side, New York, New York

Independence Place, model apartment interiors, Philadelphia, Pennsylvania

Patinkin/Grody Apartment, interior renovation, Upper West Side, New York, New York

Safra Apartment, interior renovation & furniture, Upper East Side, New York, New York

Silver Apartment, interior renovation & furniture, New York, New York

1981

Abramson Apartment, interior renovation & furniture, Upper East Side, New York, New York

Astoria Center for Motion Picture and TV, programming study, Queens, New York

Bernstein Apartment, interior renovation & furniture, New York, New York

Cavalieri, Kleier, Pearlman, office interiors & furniture, *project,* Upper East Side, New York, New York

* Film Forum 1, Soho, New York, New York (demolished)

* Gennaro Andreozzi, Inc., office interior renovation, New York, New York

Gudnason Loft, interior renovation, Chelsea, New York, New York

Mortimers, sidewalk cafe & kitchen addition, Upper East Side, New York, New York

Plotkin House, addition & interior renovation, *project,* Queens, New York

Tiger's Eye, bed and bath store renovation, New York, New York

Van Guyt Loft, interior renovation, Soho, New York, New York

1982

Ashe Darkroom, *project,* Upper East Side, New York, New York

* Balaban/Grossman Apartment, interior renovation & furniture, Upper West Side, New York, New York

Buchsbaum Loft 2, interior renovation & furniture, Soho, New York, New York

Chaplin Apartment, furniture, *project,* Upper East Side, New York, New York

Cohen Apartment, interior renovation, Upper East Side, New York, New York

Jacobson Apartment, interior renovation, New York, New York

* 6-5-4-3-2-1 Wyoming, Casa Tile '82 installation, Italian Trade Center, New York, New York

Executive Blood Stock Office, interior renovation, *project,* Soho, New York, New York

Lanning Penthouse, interior renovation & greenhouse, Upper West Side, New York, New York

* Moondance Diner, interior renovation, Soho, New York, New York

* Patricoff Kitchen, interior renovation, New York, New York

1983

Arras Gallery, interior renovation, *project,* New York, New York

* Brinkley Apartment, interior renovation & furniture, Upper West Side, New York, New York

Collect Loft, interior renovation, *project,* New York, New York

Lanning Penthouse, interior renovation, *project,* New York, New York

Morris Loft, renovation, Soho, New York, New York

* RED, for *New York Magazine,* New York, New York

Siegel Contemporary Art Gallery, interiors, Midtown, New York, New York

Siegel House, furniture, Mamaroneck, New York

* Wintour/Shaffer Townhouse, interior renovation, Soho, New York, New York

1984

* Barkin Loft, Chelsea, New York, New York

Falk House, *project,* Lawrence, New York

* Hegel's Vacation, Casa Tile '84 installation, Italian Trade Center, New York, New York

Jones/Ronson Apartment, interior renovation, Upper West Side, New York, New York

Joel House, *project,* East Marion, New York

Pear-X Table, New York, New York

* "Pencilmarkings," rug for V'Soske

Penzner Table, Soho, New York, New York

* Midler Loft, interior renovation & furniture, Tribeca, New York, New York

1985

* Dennis Apartment, interior renovation, furniture & rug, Gramercy Park, New York, New York

* Ecco Shoes, interior renovation & furniture, Chelsea, New York, New York

Elkes Interiors & Furniture, Rye, New York

* Joel/Brinkley Penthouse, interior renovation & furniture, Midtown, New York, New York

Lubin Penthouse, interior renovation & furniture, *project,* Edgewater, New Jersey

McNally Townhouse, renovation & furniture, West Village, New York, New York

* Rock Star Coffee Table, for Dennis Miller Associates

* Sugar Chair, for Dennis Miller Associates

* "Serious Leaves," rug for V'Soske

* "Pillow Rug (Hearth Rug)," rug for V'Soske

* Wintour Table, for Ecart International

1986

Cohn Apartment, furniture, Upper West Side, New York, New York

Ecco Shoes, interior renovation & furniture, Upper West Side, New York, New York

* "For Imogen," rug for V'Soske

Grey Apartment, interior renovation, Upper West Side, New York, New York

Greene Street Loft Fourth Floor, interior renovation, Soho, New York, New York

Indesign and Pisa Showroom, interior renovation, New York, New York

Jacobs Loft, interior renovation, West Village, New York, New York

Kotchoff Loft, interior renovation, *project,* New York, New York

Midler Bathroom, interior renovation, Beverly Hills, California

* Nevele Chair, for Dennis Miller Associates

* Nevele Hotel Lobby, interior renovation & furniture, Ellenville, New York

* O'Keefe Townhouse, interior renovation & furniture, Chelsea, New York, New York

1987

Ecco Shoes, interior renovation & furniture, Upper East Side, New York, New York

Kogod House, interiors, decorating & furniture, Washington, D.C.

Kron Apartment, interiors & furniture, Upper East Side, New York, New York

Nash/Strickler Apartment, *project,* Upper West Side, New York, New York

* "Rosie's Roses," rug for V'Soske

BIBLIOGRAPHY

1968
"Transparent Artistry." *House Beautiful,* Sept. 1968, 103 **(Barroon)**.

1969
"Shop Fun." *Architectural Review,* Feb. 1969, 142 **(Paper Poppy, Lucidity)**.
Smith, C. Ray. "Kinetic Boutiques and Campopop Shop." *Progressive Architecture,* Apr. 1969, 116–17 **(Paper Poppy, Lucidity)**.
"The Paper Poppy." *Japan Interior Design,* May 1969, 19–21 **(Paper Poppy)**.
"Sheet and Panel Shop Fronts." *Architectural Review,* Aug. 1969, 123–24 **(Paper Poppy)**.
"Paper Blooms at the Paper Poppy." *Greeting Card Magazine,* Sept. 1969, 14–15 **(Paper Poppy)**.

1970
"Beauty Parlour and Man's Shop." *Architectural Review,* Feb. 1970, 129–31 **(Metamorphosis)**.
"Beauty Parlor." *Japan Interior Design,* Mar. 1970, 58–60 **(Metamorphosis)**.
"Cut Out for Perfection." *Salon Owner,* Mar. 1970, 25–31 **(Metamorphosis)**.
Skurka, Norma. "The Home." *New York Times Magazine,* Sept. 27, 1970, cover, 17–19 **(Jaffee Apartment)**.
"Supergrafika." *Ameryka,* Oct. 1970, 27 **(Metamorphosis)**.

1971
"Two Baths That Turn Yesterday's Space to Today's Use." *House Beautiful,* May 1971, 94–97 **(Bathroom installation)**.
"A House Designed for Play." *House Beautiful,* July 1971, 34–39 **(Gerber House)**.
Slesin, Suzanne. "Beautiful Parlor." *Herald,* July 11, 1971, section 4 **(Metamorphosis)**.
"Westchester Cubes and Waves." *Architectural Review,* Aug. 1971, 126 **(Gerber House)**.
Skurka, Norma. "Rooms For Kids." *New York Times Magazine,* Sept. 26, 1971, 76 **(Bloch Apartment)**.

1972
Ashton, Dore. *New York: Architecture, Sculpture and Painting.* World Cultural Guides. New York: Holt, Reinholt and Winston, 1972, 196–97.
Skurka, Norma. *Underground Interiors.* New York: Quadrangle Books, 1972, 90–91.
"Exuberant Living Within Fun-Loving Forms." *House Beautiful's Building Manual,* spring/summer 1972, 106–9 **(Gerber Apartment)**.
House Beautiful, June 1972, 38 **(Lewin Apartment)**.
Lewin, Susan Grant. "Out Of Yesterday." *House Beautiful,* Sept. 1972, cover, 108–15 **(Tenenbaum Interiors)**.
Skurka, Norma. "Sunshiny Playspace." *New York Times Magazine,* Oct. 1972, 50 **(Lloyds Apartment)**.

1973
Skurka, Norma. "Ultra Renovation." *New York Times Magazine,* Feb. 4, 1973, 44–45 **(Lloyds Apartment)**.
"Fleeing From New York." *Abitare,* Mar. 1973, 202–7 **(Gerber House)**.
"An Apartment in New York." *Japan Interior Design,* May 1973, 73–76 **(Lloyds Apartment)**.
"Metamorphosis Filiale in New York." *Bauen & Wohnen,* May 1973, 180 **(Metamorphosis)**.
"Out Of a Dreamy Past." *House Beautiful,* May 1973, 96–101 **(Lewin Apartment)**.
"Functional Unit for Living." *Japan Interior Design,* Dec. 1973, 70–71 **(Here Comes Tomorrow)**.

1974
"Everything Including the Kitchen Sink." *House Beautiful,* Apr. 1974, 98–99 **(Here Comes Tomorrow)**.
"Here Comes Tomorrow." *Home Planning and Design,* summer/fall 1974, 52–53 **(Here Comes Tomorrow)**.
Conroy, Sarah Booth. "Elegant Pool." *Washington Post,* Sept. 8, 1974, K1 **(Gerber House)**.
AIA Journal, Oct. 1974, 29 **(Here Comes Tomorrow)**.
"Warm Settings For Family Meals." *McCalls,* Oct. 1974, 100 **(Lloyds Apartment kitchen)**.
"Diese Schrankwald Labt Zusammenfalten." *Zuhase,* Nov. 1974, 90–91, 93 **(Haas Apartment)**.
"Roughing It in Comfort in a Snow House." *House and Garden Second House,* fall/winter 1974–75, 24–27 **(Rosenberg House)**.

1975
"Inner Space." *W,* Feb. 7, 1975, 21 **(Haas Apartment)**.
House Beautiful's Building Manual, spring/summer 1975, 141–42.
"Reorganized Space in a City Co-op." *House and Garden Decorating Guide,* spring/summer 1975, 108–9 **(Haas Apartment)**.
House Beautiful, Apr. 1975, 69 **(Lloyds Apartment)**.

"Tailored To Taste." *House Beautiful,* May 1975, 86, 89 **(Lloyds Apartment)**.

Skurka, Norma. "Updating the Family Hearth." *New York Times Magazine,* June 15, 1975, 45 **(Shuser Kitchen)**.

Kron, Joan. "Storage as a Design Statement." *New York Magazine,* Sept. 29, 1975, 57 **(Binder Apartment)**.

"3 Manhattan Apartment Interiors." *Architectural Record,* Oct. 1975, 87, 90–91 **(Haas Apartment)**.

1976

Gueft, Olga. "Cado's New Showroom near Los Angeles." *Interiors,* Jan. 1976, 22 **(CADO Showroom)**.

American Home, Apr. 1976, 46–47 **(Lloyds Apartment)**.

Slesin, Suzanne. "Hot Tin Roofs." *New York Magazine,* Aug. 16, 1976, 47–49 **(Marantz Apartment)**.

1977

Conran, Terrance. *The Kitchen Book.* New York: Crown Publishers, 1977, 129–30, 133.

Smith, C. Ray. *Supermannerism.* New York: E. P. Dutton, 1977, 284–85.

Skurka, Norma. "Fixturing Up A Loft." *New York Times Magazine,* Feb. 6, 1977 **(Buchsbaum Loft 1)**.

Fitzgibbons, Ruth Miller. "Kitchen Design: Function With Flair." *Residential Interiors,* Mar./Apr. 1977, 69 **(Lloyds Apartment)**.

Slesin, Suzanne. "Eating in the Kitchen." *New York Magazine,* May 16, 1977, 59–63.

"Loft Living: Big Spaces, Fresh Images." *Architectural Record,* July 1977, 97–100 **(Buchsbaum Loft 1)**.

"The Wet Look." *Residential Interiors,* July/Aug. 1977, 57 **(Buchsbaum Loft 1)**.

"Art Critic's Apartment: A Factory Loft in Manhattan." *Remodeling: A House and Garden Guide,*
       fall/winter 1977, 170–74 **(Krauss Loft)**.

"Reshaping of a Co-operative." *House Beautiful's Home Remodeling,* fall/winter 1977–78, 168–71 **(Lloyds Apartment)**.

Horsley, Carter. "The Boom in Glass Bricks." *New York Times,* Nov. 17, 1977, C1, C8 **(Buchsbaum Loft 1)**.

1978

Kron, Joan, and Suzanne Slesin. *High-Tech.* New York: Clarkson N. Potter, 1978, 47, 110, 141, 155, 165, 169–70.

Szenasy, Susan. "Not Just a Plain Cupboard." *Residential Interiors,* Jan./Feb. 1978, 85 **(Cohen Interiors)**.

Slesin, Suzanne. "Finishing Touches." *New York Magazine,* Jan. 23, 1978, 58–59 **(Wahl Apartment)**.

Lewin, Susan Grant. "Designing People." *House Beautiful,* Feb. 1978, 98–99.

Kron, Joan. "Papering the Walls With Nature." *New York Times,* Mar. 23, 1978, C6 **(Miller Kitchen)**.

McMillan, Lord. "Making Room For Space." *Residential Interiors,* Mar./Apr. 1978, 68–71 **(Krauss Loft)**.

"Loft Aloft." *Ambience,* spring 1978, 36 **(Krauss Loft)**.

Haineman, Nancy. "Space Savers." *Essence,* May 1978, 136 **(Cohen Interiors)**.

"Ol Rempero Dell'arredamento Industriale." *Casa Amica,* Oct. 1978, 30–31 **(Buchsbaum Loft 1)**.

1979

"Conceptual Projects." *Urban Open Spaces.* New York: Cooper-Hewitt Museum, 1979, 21 **(The Play Setting)**.

Bennett, Janet A. "A City-Styled Country House." *Diversion,* Feb. 1979, 36S–36V **(Gerber House)**.

Horn, Richard. "Alan Buchsbaum Cabinetry." *Residential Interiors,* Mar./Apr. 1979, 80–83.

"The Recycling of America." *Time,* June 11, 1979, 84 **(Buchsbaum Loft 1)**.

"Multiply With Mirrors." *House Beautiful's Home Remodeling,* fall/winter 1979–80, 178 **(Lloyds Apartment)**.

Carlsen, Peter. "Post Modern, Life After High-Tech with Alan Buchsbaum." *Manhattan Catalogue,* Nov. 1979 **(interview)**.

Interior Design, Nov. 1979, 269 **(Cohen Interiors)**.

Bethany, Marilyn. "Fleeting Fads of 70's Decor." *New York Times Magazine,* Dec. 30, 1979, 36–37 **(Buchsbaum Loft 1)**.

1980

"Tile In Architecture." *House and Garden Building Guide.* 1980, 170–71.

Slesin, Suzanne. "Playing Up a One-Way Mirror." *New York Times,* Feb. 7, 1980, C1, C6 **(Restivo Apartment)**.

Slesin, Suzanne. "Puzzling and Seductive." *Residential Interiors,* Mar./Apr. 1980.

Bethany, Marilyn. "High-Tech Style Goes Glamorous." *New York Times Magazine,* July 20, 1980, 46–47 **(Hirsch Kitchen)**.

Lewin, Susan Grant. "A Civil War Townhouse Flourishes Anew." *House Beautiful,* Nov. 1980, 112–15 **(Center Townhouse interiors)**.

Vallifuoco, Guiseppe. "Casa Studio Per Un Architetto a New York." *L'Industrie Delle Construzioni,*
       Dec. 1980, 66–69 **(Buchsbaum Loft 1)**.

1981

Donovan, Carrie. *Living Well.* New York: New York Times Books, Pantheon Books, 1981, 12–15, 29.

Gilliat, Mary. *The Decorating Book.* New York: Pantheon Books, 1981, 98–99, 341, 347.

"Dwelling & Studio of an Architect." *Japan Interior Design,* Jan. 1981, 22, 26 **(Buchsbaum Loft 2)**.

Graaf, Vera. "Der Arkitekt, Im Still Der 50er Jahre." *Architektur & Wohnen,* Mar. 1981, 134–37 **(Buchsbaum Loft 2)**.

Lewin, Susan Grant. "Make It the Most Glamorous Room in the House." *House Beautiful,* July 1981, 58, 61 **(Hirsch Kitchen)**.

Plumb, Barbara. "Living." *Vogue,* July 1981, 65.

Byron, Elizabeth Sverbeyeff. "In an Open Space, Rooms Defined by Paint." *House and Garden,*
       Sept. 1981, 142–45 **(Sanjurjo Penthouse)**.

Miller, Nory. "Moveables." *Progressive Architecture,* Sept. 1981, 197 **(Midler vanity)**.

Demas, Renee. "New Yorker At Home." *Votre Beauté,* Oct. 1981, 126–27 **(Buchsbaum Loft 1)**.

Da Silva Ramos, Pamela. "La Coleur Advacieuse." *Paris Vogue,* Dec. 1981, 274–75 **(Buchsbaum Loft 1)**.

1982

Crane, Catherine. *Personal Places.* New York: Whitney Library of Design, 1982, 20–23.

Slesin, Suzanne. *Home.* New York: New York Times Books, 1982, 160–62, 187.

Slesin, Suzanne. "The Tile Alternative: New Design Schemes." *New York Times,* Feb. 25, 1982, C6 **(6-5-4-3-2-1 Wyoming)**.

"The Once and Future Furnishings." *Metropolis,* Apr. 1982, 3, 17 **(V'Soske Rugs)**.

Schezen, Roberto. "Cinque Lofts di Artisti Nel Cuore di Soho." *Gran Bazaar,* Apr. 1982, 100–105 **(Krauss Loft, Buchsbaum Loft 1, Buchsbaum Loft 2)**.

Wintour, Anna. "Strong Suits." *New York Magazine,* Apr. 19, 1982, 48–49.

Slesin, Suzanne. "Architects Bridge the Gap Between Home and Office." *New York Times,* May 27, 1982, C1, C12 **(Gennaro Andreozzi Office)**.

"Casa Tile '82." *New York's Inside Design,* June 1982, cover, 20–21.

Vining, Donald. "Tile's New Horizons." *Metropolitan Home,* Aug. 1982, 67.

Lloyd, Ben. "The Revisionist Loft." *Metropolitan Home,* Sept. 1982, 53–60, 62 **(Buchsbaum Loft 2)**.

Miller, Nory. "There's No Business Like Show Business." *Progressive Architecture,* Sept. 1982, 218, 221.

Seulliet, Phillipe. "Loft Story A New York." *Paris Officiel,* Sept. 1982, 340–41 **(Buchsbaum Loft 2)**.

"Combine High Tech Fixtures With High Style." *House Beautiful's Home Remodeling,* fall/winter 1982–83, 86–89 **(Hirsch Kitchen)**.

Lewin, Susan Grant. "Splendor in the Bath." *Atlanta Goodlife,* Oct. 1982, 20 **(Buchsbaum Loft 2)**.

Sisto, Maddalena. "Una Appartmento Come Un Luminoso Contenitore." *Casa Vogue,* Nov. 1982, 220–25 **(Gerber/Rothberg Apartment)**.

Bethany, Marilyn. "When Enough Is Enough." *New York Times Magazine,* Dec. 19, 1982, 98–100 **(Midler Vanity, Jakobson Bedroom)**.

1983

Clark, Sally, and Lois Perschetz. *Making Space.* New York: Clarkson N. Potter, 1983, 154–55.

Graaf, Vera. "Spiel Mit Spiegeln in Manhattan." *Architektur & Wohnen,* Jan. 1983, 34–37 **(Restivo Apartment)**.

Wintour, Anna. "One Day at a Time." *New York Magazine,* Jan. 24, 1983, 49–50 **(Gerber/Rothberg Apartment)**.

Brown, Patricia Leigh. "The Divine Mr. B." *Metropolis,* Apr. 1983, cover, 15–19.

Wintour, Anna. "All Natural, No Preservative." *New York Magazine,* Apr. 1, 1983, 48–49.

Bethany, Marilyn. "Beyond Walden." *New York Times Magazine,* June 19, 1983, 48–49.

Architects Own House of the World, July 1983, 40–41 **(Buchsbaum Loft 2)**.

"Bath 21." *Interior Design,* July 1983, 197.

Griffa, Giorgio Marie. "Still Life Da Un Interno New Yorkese." *Casa Vogue,* Sept. 1983, 312–17 **(Gerber/Rothberg Apartment)**.

McKeon, Nancy, and Corky Pollan. "Wine and Diner." *New York Magazine,* Oct. 10, 1983, 65 **(Moondance Diner)**.

Slesin, Suzanne. "The Details That Create a Fresh Look: Idiosyncratic and Elegant." *New York Times,* Oct. 27, 1983, C1, C6 **(Balaban/Grossman Apartment)**.

Da Silva, Pamela. "Elevation de Verve." *Paris Vogue,* Dec./Jan. 1983/1984, 277 **(Tenenbaum House)**.

1984

Personal Choices: A Juried Selection of Contemporary Philadelphia Architectural Drawings. Exhibition catalogue. Philadelphia: Pennsylvania Academy of the Fine Arts, 1984, 32.

Odoni, Giovanni. "Un Puzzle-Arredo Movile e Transformabile." *Casa Vogue,* Jan. 1984, 78–81 **(Balaban/Grossman Apartment)**.

Wintour, Anna. "What's Modern." *Vogue,* Jan. 1984, 180 **(interview, Balaban/Grossman table)**.

"Going Beyond Style: Young Architects and Designers." *Metropolis,* Jan./Feb. 1984.

Mazzurco, Phillip. "Entertainment Environments." *Home Entertainment,* Feb. 1984, 65 **(Lloyds Apartment)**.

Greene, Elaine. "High, Wide and Handsome." *House and Garden,* Mar. 1984, 126–31 **(Tenenbaum House)**.

Bethany, Marilyn. "Cutting-Edge Kitchen." *New York Magazine,* Apr. 2, 1984, 56–57 **(Patricoff Kitchen)**.

Brenner, Douglas. "Samuel Tenenbaum House." *Architectural Record Houses of 1983,* May 1984, 121–23 **(Tenenbaum House)**.

"The New York Look." *Metropolitan Home,* May 1984, 176, 179 **(Balaban/Grossman Apartment)**.

Brown, Kim. "House With a Heart of Steel." *Diversion,* June 1984, 58–61.

Knotos, Jason. "Live-In Kitchens." *House Beautiful,* July 1984, 58–62 **(Patricoff Kitchen)**.

Vining, Donald. "Brave New Tile." *Metropolitan Home,* Aug. 1984, 71 **(Hegel's Vacation)**.

"Interior Advantage." *Brutus,* Aug. 15, 1984, 18–21.

Morton, David. "Celebrity Homes." *Progressive Architecture,* Sept. 1984, 132–35 **(Balaban/Grossman Apartment, Brinkley Apartment)**.

Janjigian, Robert. *Autrement/New York Creation,* Oct. 1984, 142–43, 148–49 **(interview)**.

1985

Fields, Margaret. "Creating Sculpture in a City Kitchen." *Kitchen and Bath Design News,* Feb. 1985, cover, 20 **(Patricoff Kitchen)**.

Giovannini, Joseph. "Designer Rugs: Striking New Graphics for the Floor." *New York Times,* Feb. 21, 1985, C6 **(V'Soske Rugs)**.

"Die Top Ten." *Deutsch Vogue,* Mar. 1985, 24–25.

Buchsbaum, Alan. "Casa Sipario per Un'Attrice." *Casa Vogue,* June 1985, 186–89 **(Barkin Loft)**.

Greene, Elaine. "The Architect and Miss X." *House and Garden,* Nov. 1985, 210–15 **(Midler Loft)**.

1986

Krotz, Joanna. "The Revisionist Loft." *Metropolitan Home Renovation Style.* New York: Villard Books, 1986, 91–97 **(Buchsbaum Loft 2)**.

Vogel, Carol. "The Splendor of Simplicity." *New York Times Magazine,* Jan. 26, 1986, 36–40 **(Wintour/Shaffer Townhouse)**.

Von Treuenfels, Rixa. "Vogue Design." *Deutsch Vogue,* Apr. 1986, 146 **(Midler Loft)**.

Thorne, A. B. "High Tech with a Soft Touch." *Food & Wine,* June 1986, 54–58, 98 **(Hirsch Kitchen)**.

D'Arnoux, Alexandra. "American Flair." *Vogue Decoration,* Sept. 1986, 26 **(Serious Leaves Rug)**.

Fleischman, Melanie. "On the Avenue: What Makes Designers See Red." *Avenue,* Sept. 1986, 19.

Hall, Dinah. "Antennae." *World of Interiors,* Oct. 1986, 10 **(Serious Leaves Rug)**.

"Homewatch: A Focus on Chairs." *New York Newsday,* Nov. 13, 1986 **(Nevele Chair)**.

"397 Chairs Compete for a Place of Honor." *New York Times,* Nov. 13, 1986 **(Nevele Chair)**.

"Choice." *House and Garden,* Dec. 1986, 60 **(Wintour Table)**.

"New Products." *Progressive Architecture,* Dec. 1986, 116 **(Wintour Table)**.

1987

Patton, Phil. "Design on the Level: Cool Rugs by Today's Hot Architects Are Giving Floors a New Dimension." *Connoisseur,* Jan. 1987, 43–46 **(Pencilmarkings Rug)**.

Cohen, Edie Lee. "Ecco Shoes." *Interior Design,* Feb. 1987, 260–61 **(Ecco Shoes)**.

Bush, Akiko. "By Design." *Metropolis,* Mar. 1987, 64–66.

Filler, Martin. "Individualist Interiors." *House and Garden,* Mar. 1987, 64–70.

Sorkin, Michael. "Alan Buchsbaum 1935–1987." *Village Voice,* Apr. 28, 1987, 90.

"Market: Texas." *Interior Design,* June 1987, 170 **(Serious Leaves Rug)**.

Stout, Kate. "Catskill Summer." *New York Magazine,* June 15, 1987, 4A–6A **(Nevele Hotel Lobby)**.

Koncius, Jura. "User-Friendly Designs for the Office." *Washington Post,* Washington Home section, June 18, 1987, cover, 17–18 **(Wintour Table)**.

Filler, Martin. "Eye of his Times." *Architectural Record,* mid-Sept. 1987, 108–19 **(Nevele Hotel Lobby, Joel/Brinkley Penthouse, O'Keefe Townhouse)**.

Filler, Martin. "Journal: The Boom Boom Room." *House and Garden,* Nov. 1987 **(Nevele Hotel Lobby)**.

1988

Architectural League of New York. *397 Chairs.* New York: Harry N. Abrams, 1988, 61 **(Nevele Chair)**.

"New and Refinished Flooring Brings Buildings New Life." *Floor Covering Weekly,* Feb. 1988, A8 **(Nevele Hotel Lobby)**.

Weiner, Ellis. "Last Resort: Dressed to Catskill." *Metropolitan Home,* Oct. 1988, 76B–78 **(Nevele Hotel Lobby)**.

Brown, Patricia Leigh. "Currents: Designers' Saturday: Chairs, Beds, Tables and Tired Feet." *New York Times,* Oct. 13, 1988, C3 **(Nevele Furniture Collection)**.

Bush, Akiko. "Landscapes of the Fantastic." *Metropolis,* Nov. 1988, 62–67, 71, 75 **(Nevele Hotel Lobby)**.

1989

"Hot Properties." *Metropolitan Home,* May 1989, 184 **(Nevele Chair)**.

"Market." *Interior Design,* July 1989, 86 **(Nevele Chair)**.

1990

Staebler, Wendy. *Architectural Detailing in Residential Interiors.* New York: Whitney Library of Design, 1990, 114–15 **(O'Keefe Townhouse)**.

1991

Michel, Florence. *Architecture Interieure Crée,* Apr./May 1991, 154–55 **(Nevele Hotel Lobby)**.

1992

Schwartz, Frederic, and Cornelia Groethuysen. "Hotel Lobby in Ellenville." *Baumeister,* Nov. 1992, 38–39 **(Nevele Hotel Lobby)**.

1994

Design Legacies: A Tribute to Architects and Designers Who Have Died of AIDS. Exhibition catalog, 1994, 4.

1995

Stern, Robert A. M., Thomas Mellins, and David Fishman. *New York 1960: Architecture and Urbanism Between the Second World War and the Bicentennial.* New York: The Monacelli Press, 1995, 596–97 **(Paper Poppy)**.